CONTE

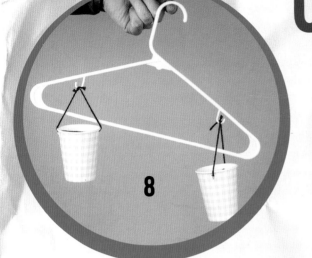

8

34

54

MW01155655

INTRODUCTION

Long before people had written language, they had math. To keep track of objects, they carved marks on tally sticks made of bone or stone. As time passed, people began to develop a greater understanding of math and how it could be used to help them make calculations, build structures, and keep track of the sky and the seasons.

Today, you can use paper and pencil to make tally marks. 20,000 years ago, people carved tally marks into bone.

Written by Nicole Sulgit and Beth Taylor
Photo styling by Nick LaShure and Nicole Sulgit
Photography by Christopher Hiltz, Nick LaShure and Nicole Sulgit
Additional images from Shutterstock.com

First printing
Manufactured in China.
03/2021 Guangdong

8 7 6 5 4 3 2 1

SAFETY WARNING
All of the experiments and activities in this book MUST be performed with adult supervision. All projects contain a degree of risk, so carefully read all instructions before you begin and make sure that you have safety materials such as goggles, gloves, etc. Also make sure that you have safety equipment, such as a fire extinguisher and first aid kit, on hand. You are assuming the risk of any injury by conducting these activities and experiments. Publications International, Ltd. will not be liable for any injury or property damage.

Let's get social!
⬤ @Publications_International
⬤ @PublicationsInternational
⬤ @BrainGames.TM
www.pilbooks.com

BRANCHES OF MATHEMATICS

Arithmetic is one branch of mathematics. Students learn a lot of arithmetic when they learn addition, subtraction, multiplication, and division.

Geometry, another branch of math, looks at questions of space and shapes such as how volume can be determined.

MATH AND SCIENCE

Physics is a branch of science that studies matter, energy, and the fundamental forces of the universe. Math and physics are closely tied together. As Isaac Newton was studying how motion, gravity, and force worked, he also was advancing the field of modern calculus, a branch of mathematics that studies change over time.

IN THIS BOOK

In the experiments in this book, you'll be using numbers to make measurements, learning more about geometry and shapes, and examining the forces that affect movement under water and in the air. Let's get started!

MEASUREMENTS

There have been many systems of measurement used throughout history. In ancient times, people needed ways to trade goods, to build houses and navigate on boats, and to record rainfall and the levels of rivers and streams.

Royal Cubit

ANCIENT SYSTEMS OF MEASUREMENT

A number of ancient civilizations used a measurement called the cubit. A cubit in ancient Egypt wasn't the same length as a cubit in ancient Greece or ancient Rome, though. The length of a cubit varied from culture to culture and over time, although it often corresponded roughly to the approximate length of a person's elbow to the tip of their middle finger.

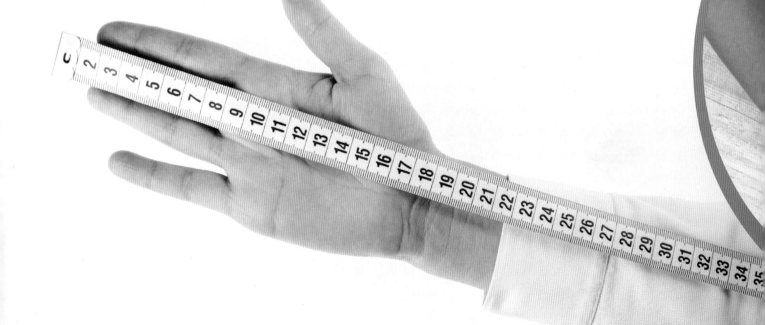

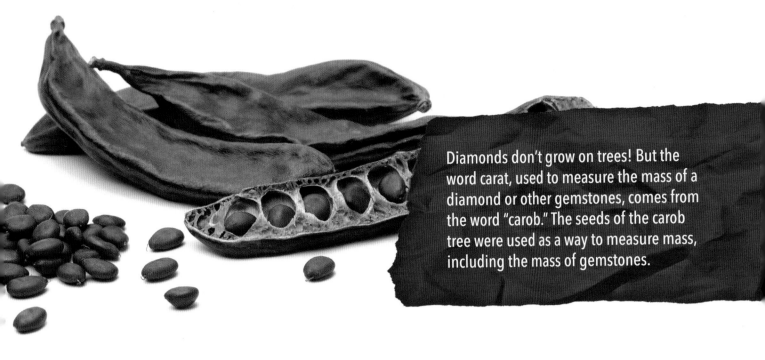

Diamonds don't grow on trees! But the word carat, used to measure the mass of a diamond or other gemstones, comes from the word "carob." The seeds of the carob tree were used as a way to measure mass, including the mass of gemstones.

MODERN SYSTEMS OF MEASUREMENT

The International System of Units is also called the metric system. It defines seven "base units" and then measures everything in comparison to them. For example, a meter is used to define length. A meter is the distance traveled by light in a vacuum during a time interval of 1/299792458 of a second.

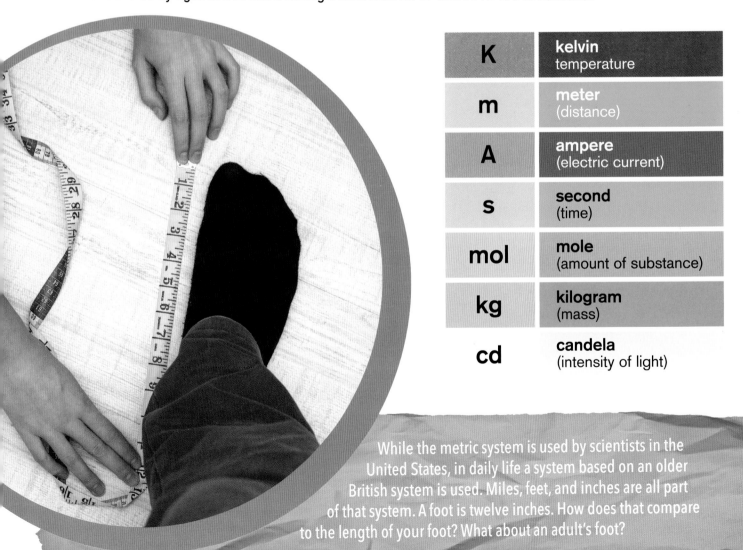

K	kelvin temperature
m	meter (distance)
A	ampere (electric current)
s	second (time)
mol	mole (amount of substance)
kg	kilogram (mass)
cd	candela (intensity of light)

While the metric system is used by scientists in the United States, in daily life a system based on an older British system is used. Miles, feet, and inches are all part of that system. A foot is twelve inches. How does that compare to the length of your foot? What about an adult's foot?

BUILD YOUR OWN SCALE

You can create your own scale to determine whether one object is lighter or heavier than another.

MATERIALS

- Yarn
- Scissors
- Two paper cups
- Hanger
- Ruler
- Small objects such as beans or seeds

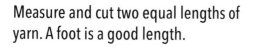

Step 1

Measure and cut two equal lengths of yarn. A foot is a good length.

Step 2

Carefully poke two holes in each cup.

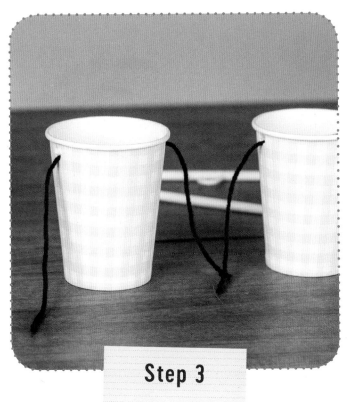

Step 3

Thread one piece of yarn through each cup.

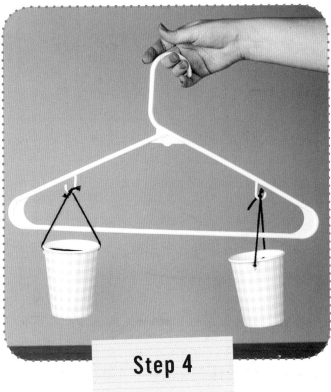

Step 4

Tie the cups to each side of the hanger.

Step 5

Pour the beans or seeds into one cup.

Step 6

The hanger will tilt downward. You can balance it again by putting beans in the other cup.

LATITUDE LOCATOR

If you look at a globe, you will see an overlay of imaginary lines. People use them to assign each place a set of geographic coordinates.

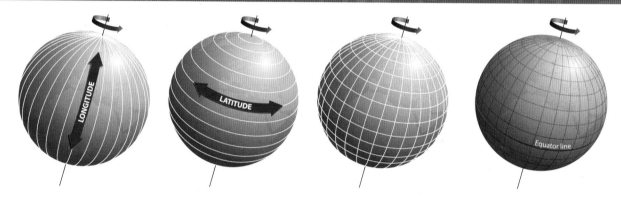

The horizontal lines mark latitude. The equator is at 0 degrees, with the North Pole at 90 degrees North and the South Pole at 90 degrees South. The vertical lines mark longitude. Longitude marks the distance East or West from a line called the Prime Meridian.

MATERIALS

- Protractor
- Tape
- String
- A small weight
- Scissors
- Straw

You can find your latitude location with very simple tools—and the help of the North Star. The angle at which the North Star rises above the horizon corresponds to your latitude. At the equator, latitude 0 degrees, the North Star can be seen on the horizon. At the North Pole, latitude 90 degrees, you would have to look straight up to find the North Star.

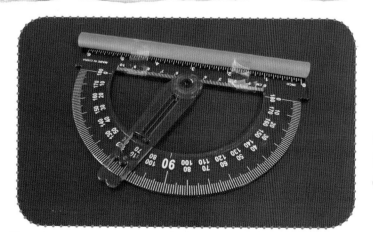

Step 1

Cut the straw to the length of the protractor and tape it on. This will act as a sight that will help you focus on the North Star.

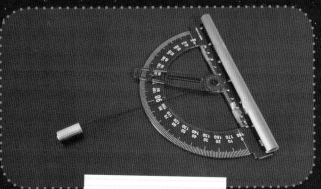

Step 2

Step 3

Thread a string tied to a small weight through the small hole in the protractor.

The weight needs to hang freely.

With an adult, go outside at night and find the North Star. Tilt the protractor up to peer at the North Star through the straw. Note where the string crosses the protractor.

The protractor has two lines of numbers: running from 0 at the side to 90 at the bottom, and running from 180 at the side to 90 at the bottom. At the equator, 0 degrees, if you were looking straight ahead at the North Star, your string would cross the 90 on the protractor. At the North Pole, 90 degrees North, you would have to tilt your protractor straight up, and the string would cross the 180 mark.

To get your latitude, just subtract 90 from the larger number and you have your latitude!

Ursa Minor
(Little Dipper)

Polaris
(North Star)

Ursa Major
(Big Dipper)

RAIN GAUGE

How much rain does your area get? Measure over time with this simple rain gauge.

- Large bottle
- Small bottle
- Measuring cup
- Gravel or pebbles
- Scissors
- Ruler
- Tape

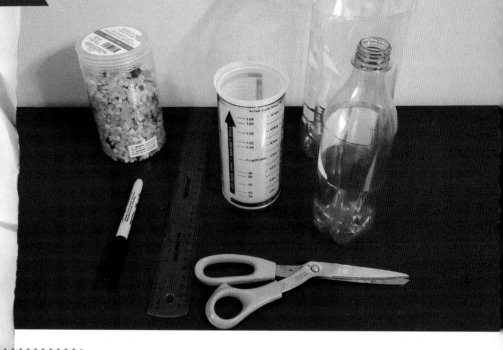

Step 1

Cut the tops off both bottles.

Step 2

Using the measuring cup, pour a quarter cup of water into the smaller bottle. Mark increments as you pour each half cup in.

Step 3

Add gravel to the bottom of the larger bottle to weigh down your rain gauge.

Step 4

Place the smaller bottle into the larger one.

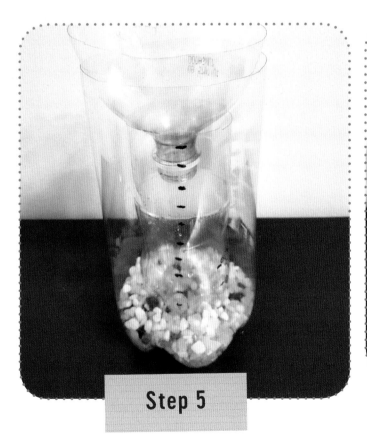

Step 5

Use the top of the larger bottle as a funnel.

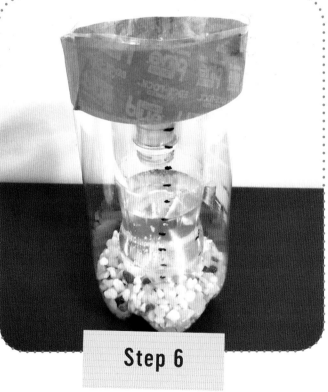

Step 6

Tape the funnel into place to secure it. Place the rain gauge where it can gather water!

GRAVITY

Gravity is a force that pulls matter together. Every object has gravity. You have gravity!

Objects with more matter have more gravity. Compared to you, the Earth has a much bigger gravitational pull. When you throw a ball in the air, it returns to the ground instead of floating in midair or bumping into you because of Earth's gravitational pull.

OUR MASSIVE SUN

The Sun has more mass than the Earth. The mass of the Sun is equivalent to the mass of 333,000 Earths. The Sun's gravitational pull keeps the Earth in orbit around it.

So if the Earth has less mass than the Sun, why does our Moon orbit the Earth instead of the Sun? It's because of distance. When an object is closer, it will exert a stronger gravitational pull. The Moon stays in orbit around the Earth because of Earth's gravitational pull. And the Moon exerts a gravitational pull on the Earth, too, that's reflected in the movement of the ocean tides.

Do heavier objects fall faster?

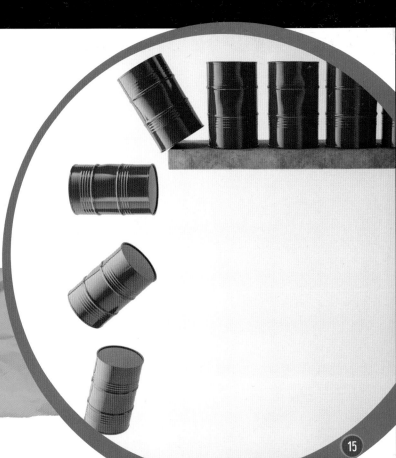

We know that objects fall towards the Earth because of gravity. Do objects with more mass fall faster to the ground? Let's turn the page and do an experiment to see.

BINDER CLIP VS. NAPKIN

A binder clip weighs more than a napkin. Will it fall faster? Let's see.

MATERIALS

- Three napkins
- Two binder clips

You can do this experiment with any objects you have around the house. Paper towels or printer paper can substitute for napkins, while pebbles or grapes can substitute for binder clips.

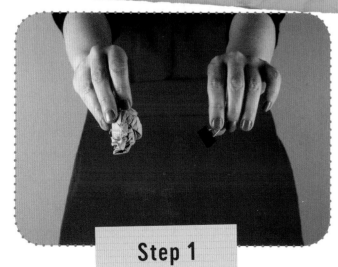

Step 1

Crumple up a napkin. Hold it and a binder clip or other small, dense object at the same height.

Step 2

Let them drop. What happens? They fall at the same speed. Gravity exerts the same force on both objects, regardless of mass.

Now let's see if we can introduce another element, that of air resistance. This time, use a napkin that is not crumpled.

While gravity pushes down on both objects, air resistance exerts a greater effect on the wide surface area of the napkin. It falls more slowly.

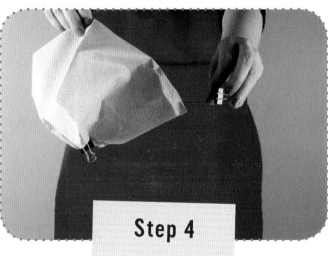

Step 4

You can create a makeshift parachute using a napkin and a second binder clip.

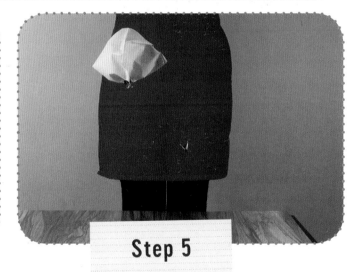

Step 5

The binder clip with the napkin "parachute" attached will fall more slowly than the binder clip by itself.

HOW DOES IT WORK?

Wide shapes such as parachutes maximize air resistance, countering the force of gravity.

PARACHUTES

When a skydiver jumps out of a plane, they immediately begin to fall. In the first part of a skydive, the freefall, the parachute is not yet deployed. The skydiver accelerates as they fall, eventually reaching a speed called terminal velocity. This is the greatest speed they will achieve. At this speed, the forces of gravity (weight) and its countering force drag (air resistance) balance each other out. Then the skydiver deploys the parachute to slow down their speed for a safe landing.

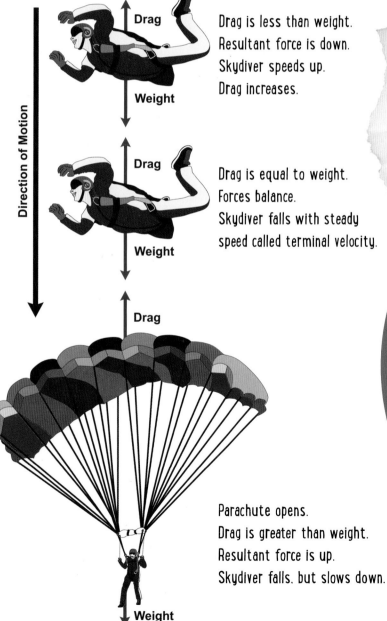

Direction of Motion

Drag

Weight

Drag is less than weight.
Resultant force is down.
Skydiver speeds up.
Drag increases.

Drag

Weight

Drag is equal to weight.
Forces balance.
Skydiver falls with steady
speed called terminal velocity.

Drag

Parachute opens.
Drag is greater than weight.
Resultant force is up.
Skydiver falls, but slows down.

Weight

Because we can't see it, we often think of air as nothing. But air acts as a fluid, a substance that flows.

The shape of a parachute's canopy is carefully tailored to provide air resistance. Many parachutes today use a rectangular configuration known as a ram-air design. These are easier to control than traditional round chutes.

Many skydivers can work together to create incredible formations.

PAPER CUP PARACHUTE

Make a parachute and test it outdoors!

MATERIALS

- Plastic bag
- Scissors
- Paper cup
- Ribbon or yarn
- Small objects such as clothespins

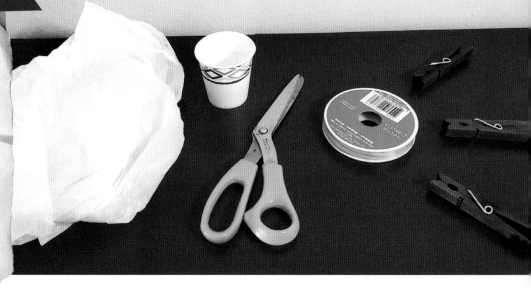

Step 1

Cut a square from the top of the plastic bag.

Step 2

Use the tips of the scissors to carefully poke four holes at the top of the cup, at equal distances from each other.

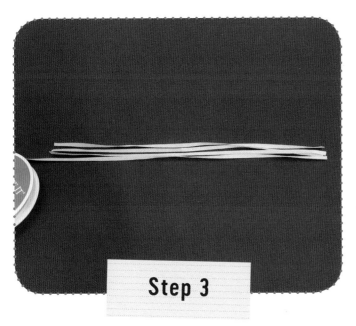

Step 3

Cut four lengths of ribbon. Once you've cut one, you can measure the other three against that length of ribbon so they are all the same in length.

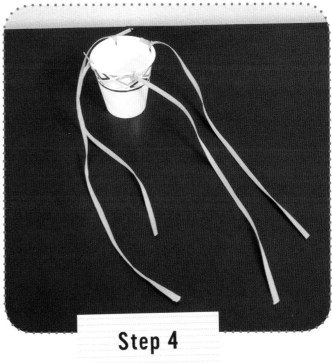

Step 4

Thread each piece of ribbon through a hole in the cup. Knot it securely.

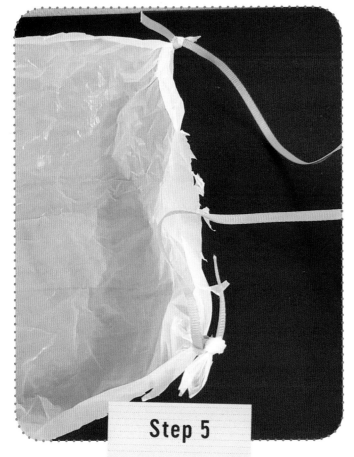

Step 5

Secure each piece of ribbon to one corner of the plastic.

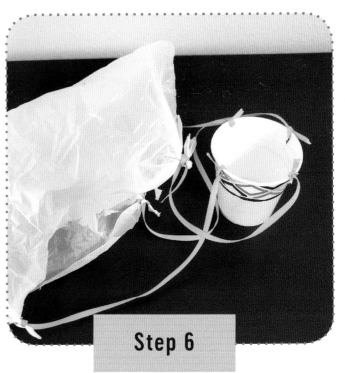

Step 6

Drop your parachute from a balcony, second story window, or the top of a flight of steps to see how long it takes to reach the ground. Add small objects to see how much the parachute can carry. Take care not to drop your parachute on anything underneath.

MACHINES AND TOOLS

What pops into your head when you hear the word "machine"? Maybe you think of a washing machine, a robot, or a furnace—something complex, with many mechanical parts. But some machines are very simple. They're so basic you may not think of them as machines at all!

SIX SIMPLE MACHINES

The six "simple machines" are the inclined plane, the wedge, the lever, the wheel and axle, the pulley, and the screw. Each of these machines helps humans do work. To scientists, "work" doesn't mean something like doing your homework. Work is done when someone—or something—applies a force that moves an object over a distance. When you throw a ball, you are doing work. Simple machines make it easier for you to do work.

Throwing a ball is work!

When you go up a ramp, you are using a machine—an **inclined plane**. It's easier to push an object up a ramp than it is to lift it straight up.

When you apply a force to one end of the **wedge**, it transports that force to the sharp edge of the wedge.

Have you played on a seesaw? Then you've used a **lever**! A lever has two parts: one long part such as a beam rests on a support, called a fulcrum. You apply force to one side of the lever to move it. In the picture, a painter uses a screwdriver as a lever to open the paint can. The edge of the paint can acts as a fulcrum. In the last experiment, the scale was a lever that balanced on a central fulcrum.

A steering wheel is an example of a wheel and axle. Connect a cylinder, or rod, to a wheel to form this simple machine.

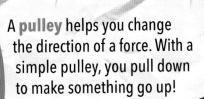

A **pulley** helps you change the direction of a force. With a simple pulley, you pull down to make something go up!

The edges on **screws** are called threads.

RAMP

You can create an inclined plane with simple household objects.

MATERIALS

- Books
- Sturdy cardboard (we used the cardboard from the back of a legal pad)
- Toy car or truck

Step 1

Set up a shallow ramp.

Step 2

Hold the toy car at the top of the ramp.

Step 3

Let it go. How fast and how far does it go?

Step 4   Make your ramp steeper. How does this affect the car's speed and distance?

 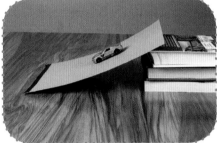 

Step 5   Make your ramp even steeper. How does this affect the car's speed and distance?

Step 6   At what point is the ramp so steep that the car cannot make it safely down the ramp?

On mountains, roads need to be built so that cars can make it up and down safely. You'll see a switchback formation rather than a straight, steep road.

DRAWBRIDGE

Create a simple pulley system to raise
and lower your castle drawbridge.

MATERIALS

- Box
- Yarn
- Ruler
- Scissors
- Marker or pen
- Toy soldiers or princesses. animal figures. or toy cars (optional)

Step 1

Cut any flaps or lids off the box.

Step 2

Using the ruler and pen or marker, outline a rectangular shape on the box.

Step 3

Ask an adult for help with this step! Cut a flap in the box. Use the tips of the scissors or a hole punch to make two small holes, one on the top left corner of the flap and the other on the top right.

Step 4

Measure two lengths of string or yarn, each about 36 inches (91 cm) long.

Step 5

Thread the yarn through the holes in the flaps.

Step 6

You can now raise and lower your drawbridge, letting in—or keeping out—soldiers, cars, or other figures!

COIN SORTER

Sort objects based on size with this easy machine that uses gravity to do its work.

MATERIALS

- Empty tissue box
- Cardboard tube
- Sturdy tape
- Scissors
- Ruler or measuring tape
- Pen or pencil
- Coins

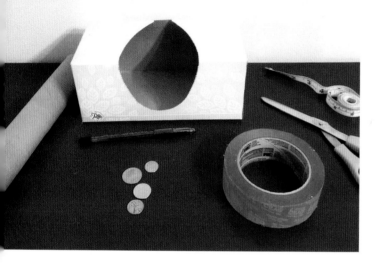

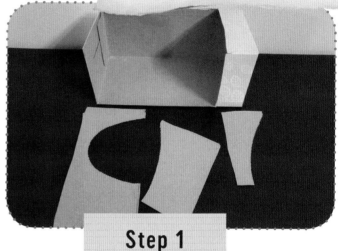

Step 1

Cut off the top and front panels of the tissue box, leaving a bit of a ledge on one side for the chute to rest against.

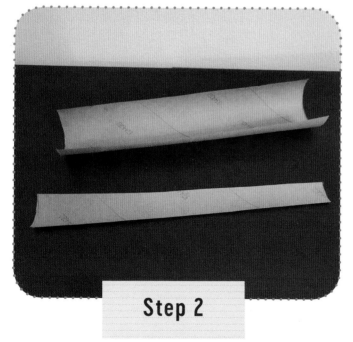

Step 2

Cut a section out of the cardboard tube so you're left with a slightly-curved chute.

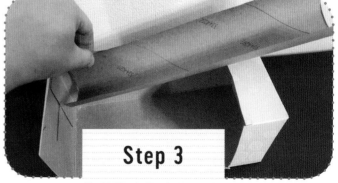

Step 3

Hold the chute against the tissue box to get an idea of where you will cut the three holes in steps 4 and 5. The largest coins, the quarters, will fall off the end of the chute.

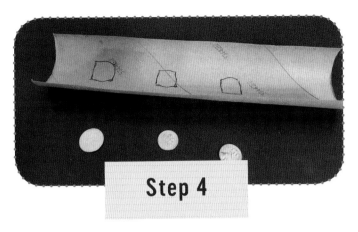

Step 4

Draw a square outline around each coin. You will need to be precise, as coins are very similar in size. Use a ruler or measuring tape to make sure the holes are accurate and in a row.

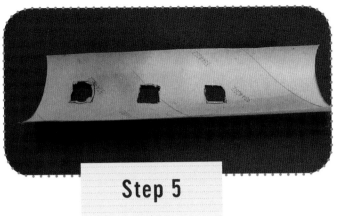

Step 5

Cut out the outlines for each coin. It is probably easiest to score the cardboard with one end of the scissors and then carefully punch out the hole. Ask an adult for help with this step.

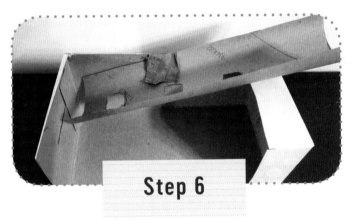

Step 6

Tape the chute in place. Remember to leave a little space at the end for the quarter to fall through. The hole for the smallest coin is at the top of the chute.

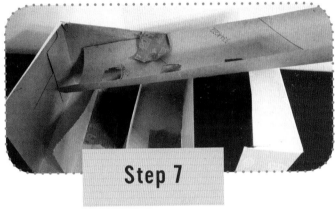

Step 7

Using the leftover cardboard from step 1, tape panels between the holes to the bottom of the box to create compartments that separate the coins.

Step 8

Hold a coin at the top and let it slide down the chute! The smaller coins will fall through the smaller holes at the top of the chute, while the larger ones will skate on by.

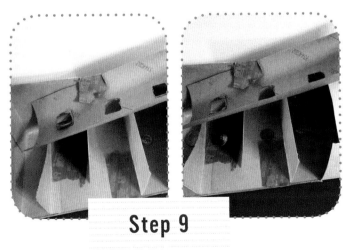

Step 9

If your coin sorter isn't working, you may need to widen the holes or narrow them by adding a piece of tape to one side.

WHEELBARROW

Pushing a load makes it easier to move than carrying it. Try it out with a wheelbarrow.

MATERIALS

- Cardboard box
- 2 long or 4 short pieces of wood
- Short pencil
- Spool
- Tape
- Scissors

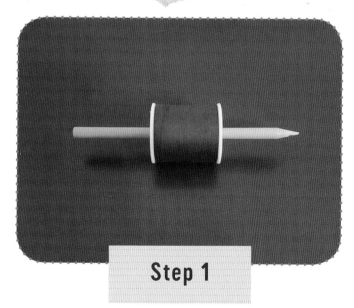

Step 1

The spool will be the wheel of your wheelbarrow. Thread the pencil through the hole.

Step 2

Tape the wooden strips to the box.

Step 3

Secure the ends of the wooden strips to the ends of the pencil with tape.

Step 4

Use your wheelbarrow!

Wheels are a type of lever. You apply the force to the handles, and the wheel acts as the fulcrum to move the load.

SHAPES AND STRUCTURES

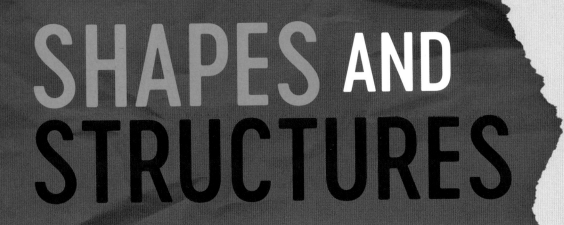

Geometry, a branch of mathematics, helps you learn about shapes—not just squares and circles, but three-dimensional shapes like cones, cylinders, and spheres. People use geometry when they're trying to figure out how much can fit in a box, or how much paint to buy to paint a room in their house.

HOW MANY SIDES?

Most buildings have four sides, but the Pentagon is in the shape of a five-sided pentagon. Originally, it was going to be built in a different location, on a piece of land with roughly five sides, so the design matched the space. Even when a different location was chosen, the five-sided design was still used.

Euclid, who lived in ancient Greece, is considered the father of geometry. He wrote a book about math called *Elements* that was used for centuries.

Shapes can be used in art and design. This type of pattern is called a tessellation.

TOOTHPICK S.T.E.M. STRUCTURES

Build 3-D shapes using toothpicks and gumdrops, mini marshmallows, or balls of modeling clay. Then record the number of faces, edges, and vertices of each shape in an observation notebook. Faces are the shape's surfaces. Edges are the line segments where two faces meet. Vertices are the points or corners where edges meet.

MATERIALS

- Toothpicks
- Gumdrops
- Observation notebook

CUBE

Step 1

Form a square for the base with 4 toothpicks and a gumdrop in each of the 4 corners. You can also use mini marshmallows or balls of modeling clay.

Stick another toothpick into the top of each gumdrop. The new toothpicks should stand upright on top of the square base.

Step 2

Step 3

Create another square as you did in step 1. Position the second square on top of the vertical toothpicks and connect to complete the cube. *How many faces, edges, and vertices does the cube have?* Record results in your observation notebook.

SQUARE PYRAMID

A pyramid is a solid shape that rises to a single point. All of the faces (sides) that are not the base must be triangles.

Step 1

Form a square for the base with 4 toothpicks and 4 gumdrops.

Step 2

Stick a toothpick into each gumdrop of the base at an angle so that the ends meet in the center.

Step 3

Connect the unattached ends of the toothpicks to another gumdrop to complete the square pyramid. *How many faces, edges, and vertices does the square pyramid have?* Record results in your observation notebook.

TRIANGULAR PRISM

A prism has the same top and bottom shape,
connected by rectangles or parallelograms.

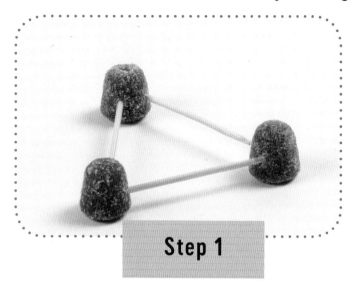

Step 1

Form a triangle for the base with
3 toothpicks and 3 gumdrops.

Step 2

Stick another toothpick into the top of each
gumdrop. The new toothpicks should stand upright
on top of the square base.

Step 3

Make another triangle as you did in
step 1. Position the second triangle on
top of the vertical toothpicks and connect
to complete the triangular prism. *How
many faces, edges, and vertices does the
triangular prism have?* Record results in
your observation notebook.

TIP:

Your S.T.E.M. structures will be strongest if you stick the toothpicks into the gumdrops at the correct
angle and don't reposition them. Forming a 2-D shape with toothpicks alone (and no gumdrops) first
helps you see the correct angles. Once you've inserted a toothpick at the angle you want, push the
toothpick almost all the way through the gumdrop.

STANDING ON EGGS

Will eggs break if you stand on them? Try it and see!
(Wash your feet before and after doing this.)

MATERIALS

- 1 or 2 cartons of raw eggs

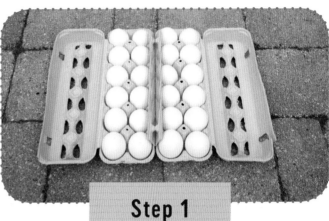

Step 1

Open the cartons and place them side-by-side. Take off your shoes so you are barefoot.

Step 3

Do they break?
Why not?

Step 2

Have someone help you step up on the eggs.

Part of the answer has to do with the shape of the egg. Eggs are arches, which are strong shapes that can support a lot of weight. They are a common bridge shape for that reason.

PAPER TOWER

How high can you build a tower made only from paper and tape?

MATERIALS

- Printer paper
- Masking or clear tape

Step 1

Make a cylindrical roll from a piece of paper. Make sure the ends are lined up neatly.

Step 2

Tape the paper into place.

Step 3

Make two more rolls to form the base of the tower.

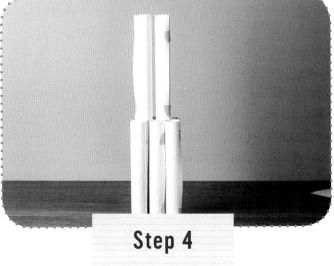

Step 4

Now comes the hard part–form a new row by balancing two more rolls of paper on top.

Step 5

Now comes the trickiest part of all. Can you add one more roll to the very top?

FOR AN EXTRA CHALLENGE

In our first example, we rolled each paper along the short side. Let's try rolling along the long side this time. Adding a flat piece of paper between rows may help.

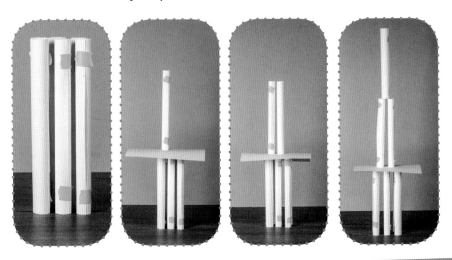

FURTHER EXPERIMENTATION

Vary the size of the cylindrical rolls to see if it helps you make the structure more or less sound. Try this experiment on different surfaces to see if one works better than others. If you use more than three cylindrical rolls for the bottom base, how high can your tower go?

HOUSE OF CARDS

With care, precision, and a little bit of luck, you can build a very high structure from flimsy paper cards.

MATERIALS

- A deck of cards, preferably an older one
- A flat surface. Surfaces with texture will work better than smooth ones.

Step 1

Prop two cards against each other.

Step 2

Prop two more cards against each other.

Step 3

Balance a card on top of your two triangular pyramids.

Step 4

Balance two more cards in a pyramid above it.

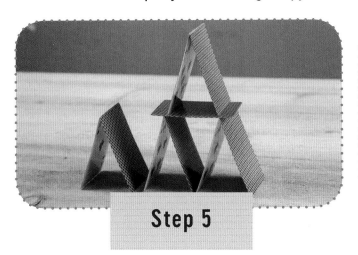

Step 5

You can expand your house by building to the left or right.

Step 6

With a wider base, you can build your house higher as well.

This is the basic structure of your house of cards. See how tall you can build your house!

DID YOU KNOW?

In 2007, a man named Bryan Berg set the Guiness World Record for the tallest house of cards. It was more than 25 feet (7.8 meters) tall!

IN THE WATER

We spend most of our lives on land, but about 70 percent of Earth's surface is covered by water. Water and other liquids can exhibit fascinating, unexpected behavior. There is even a branch of physics called fluid mechanics that examines how liquids, gases, and plasmas work.

BUOYANCY

Some objects float and some objects sink. The force of gravity works to push an object downward. The force of buoyancy pushes an object upward. If an object is more dense than the liquid, it will sink. Objects that are less dense will float. That does not depend on the size of the object or how heavy it is. While we might expect that big objects will sink and smaller objects will float, that is not true. Otherwise a coin would float when you toss it in a fountain, and large ships would sink.

Buoys—floating objects that act as markers—are buoyant!

ARCHIMEDES'S PRINCIPLE

When you put something in water, it displaces the water—that is, it moves it. Thousands of years ago, a man named Archimedes of Syracuse described a law of physics. He said that an object is buoyed up by a force equal to the weight of the water it displaces. If the force is strong enough—if enough water is displaced—the object floats.

Scuba divers use something called a buoyancy control device (BCD) to help them stay at the depth they want to stay at.

WALKING WATER

Do you think you can get water to defy gravity and walk from one glass to another? Try this experiment to find out!

MATERIALS

- 5 clear glasses
- Food coloring in 3 colors
- 4 half-sheet paper towels
- Spoon
- Water
- Scissors

Step 1

Line up 5 clear glasses in a row. We are using 9-ounce plastic glasses. Fill the first, third, and fifth glasses about ¾ full with water.

Step 2

Add a few drops of food coloring to each water-filled glass, using a different color for each. Stir with a spoon until well blended. Clean the spoon after each glass to prevent color transfers.

Step 3

Fold each half-sheet paper towel like an accordion into a strip about 1 inch wide.

Step 4

Fold each strip in half to form a V shape. The V should be a little taller than the glasses. Trim any excess off the paper towel ends.

Step 5

Flip the V shape upside down. Place one end in a glass with colored water and the other end in an adjacent empty glass.

Step 6

Repeat with the other glasses in the row, placing a paper towel strip between each pair of adjacent glasses.

Step 7

Take a break! This experiment moves very slowly, so you can check back later. *What do you observe after 30 minutes? What do you observe the next day?*

HOW DOES IT WORK?

The water moves up the paper towels (seeming to defy gravity) through a process called capillary action. Water gets pulled into the tiny gaps between the fibers of the paper towels and eventually down into the empty glasses. The gaps in the paper towel act like capillary tubes and pull the water upward. This process is what helps water travel up from the roots of a plant to the rest of the plant.

SOAP BOAT

Can you move a paper boat forward using nothing but soap?

MATERIALS

- Cardstock
- Scissors
- Toothpick
- Dishwashing liquid
- Shallow tray or container of water

Step 1

Cut out a boat shape from the cardstock. The front of the boat has a point like the roof of a house, and the back of the boat has a notch cut out.

Step 2

Fill a shallow tray or container with water. Place your boat on the surface at one end and point it forward. Act quickly before the paper boat starts to curl! Dip a toothpick in dishwashing liquid.

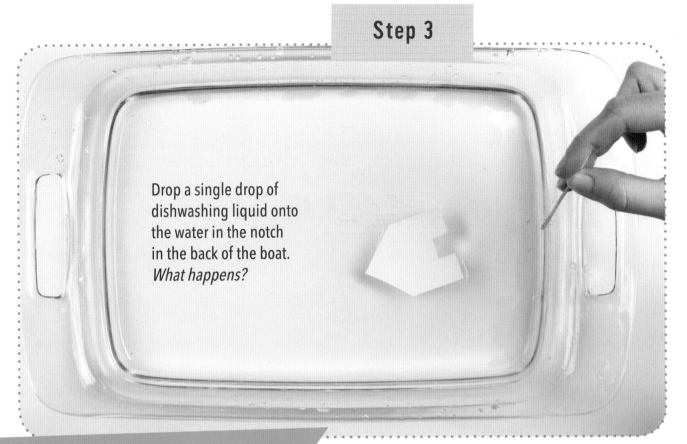

Drop a single drop of dishwashing liquid onto the water in the notch in the back of the boat. *What happens?*

HOW DOES IT WORK?

The paper boat moves due to a force called surface tension. Water molecules are strongly attracted and cling close together, especially on the surface. This attraction creates surface tension. Adding soap to the water weakens the bonds behind the boat, reducing surface tension. As a result, the rest of the water surface pulls away, dragging the boat along with it.

These bugs, called water striders, stay on top of water because of surface tension. Their long, thin legs keep their weight balanced as they move lightly across the water.

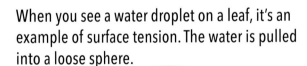

When you see a water droplet on a leaf, it's an example of surface tension. The water is pulled into a loose sphere.

47

LOAD A BOAT

Aluminum foil seems like it would make a flimsy boat—but it can carry more than you think!

MATERIALS

- Bowl of water
- Aluminum foil
- Pennies or other small objects that act as "cargo" for your boat

Step 1

Tear off a sheet of aluminum foil for your boat.

Step 2

Fold it in half. Turn it up at the edges to make a small square with raised edges.

Step 3

Place your boat in the water.

Step 4

Begin loading the cargo in your boat.

CAN YOU GET YOUR BOAT TO SINK?

  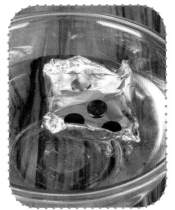 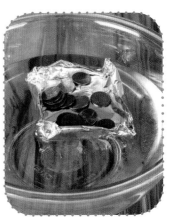

NOW, EXPERIMENT!

Will a larger, wider boat carry more? What if you use a double sheet of foil?

49

SODA CAN SUBMARINE

Submarines control how they rise and fall through the use of air. See how it works in this experiment.

MATERIALS

- Empty soda can
- Short length of tubing
- Container full of water, deeper than the soda can

Step 1

Fill the soda can with water and insert the tube into the can.

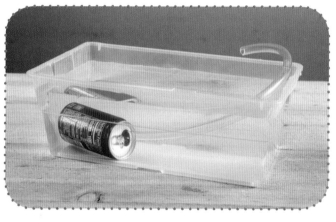

Step 2

Submerge the submarine. If it rises to the surface, add more water into the soda can so it is completely full and sinks. Leave the other end of the tubing above the water.

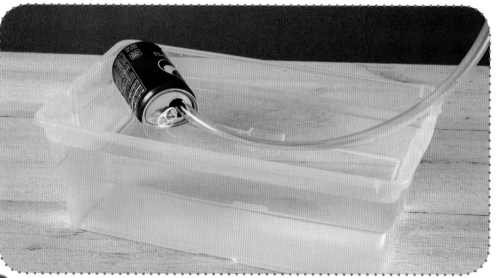

Step 3

Blow into the tube. As air travels along the tube and fills the can, the can rises again.

SUBMARINES

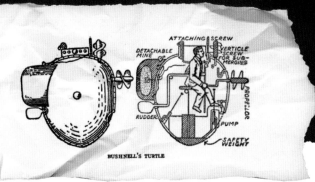

BUSHNELL'S TURTLE

Submarines have been around for a long time. In fact, an inventor named David Bushnell invented a kind of submarine that was used during the American Revolutionary War! He called it the *Turtle*. Submarines today look a lot different. Modern submarines are powered by engines or nuclear power.

Submarines have tanks of water called ballast. Water weighs the submarine down as it submerges. Water is released from the tank when it is ready to rise. Propellers move the submarine forward.

Submarines can hold a lot of people. On a nuclear-powered submarine used by the military, the crew can consist of more than 100 people.

IN THE AIR

Orville and Wilbur Wright took their first successful flight at Kitty Hawk in 1903. Since then, planes have grown larger and faster. But planes weren't the first airborne objects. People had been using hang gliders and balloons long before the Wright Brothers were born. How have humans managed to keep objects in the air? They have come to an understanding of four forces that affect airplane flight: weight, lift, thrust, and drag.

WEIGHT

If you jump in the air, you will return to the Earth. That's the force of gravity, or weight, acting on you. Weight acts on airplanes, balloons, and kites too.

LIFT

Lift pushes an object upward, countering its weight. The wings of an airplane are instrumental in keeping it aloft. They are shaped so that the air pressure underneath the wing is higher than the pressure above the wing, which helps keep the airplane up. If you are on an airplane, you may see flaps extend or retract during the flight, especially during takeoff or landing. Changes in the shape of the wing help control the airplane.

THRUST

Thrust is the force that sets the airplane in motion and keeps it moving in the right direction. In airplanes, engines produce thrust. When you throw a paper airplane, you are providing thrust.

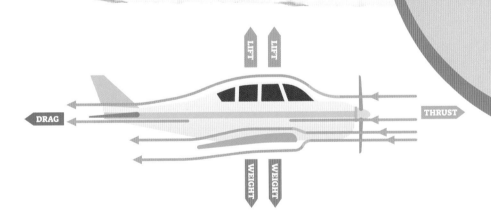

DRAG

Just as weight and lift are opposite forces, thrust and drag are opposite forces. Drag works to slow an aircraft down.

AIR VORTEX CANNON

Create an air vortex cannon—a simple device that shoots out bursts of air. Then test how far you can shoot air from your cannon.

MATERIALS

- Paper or plastic cup
- Rubber band
- Balloon
- Scissors
- Craft knife
- Tape
- Toilet paper
- Measuring tape

Step 1

With an adult's help, use a craft knife or scissors to cut a circular hole in the bottom of the cup. We are using a 9-ounce paper cup.

Step 2

Inflate the balloon to stretch it out, then deflate it. Tie a knot in the neck of the deflated balloon.

Step 3

Use scissors to cut off the top of the balloon, on the opposite side as the tied neck.

Step 4

Stretch the balloon over the top of the cup, with the tied neck facing outward and the excess balloon overlapping on all sides.

Step 5

Wrap a rubber band around the top of the cup to secure the balloon beneath the lip of the cup.

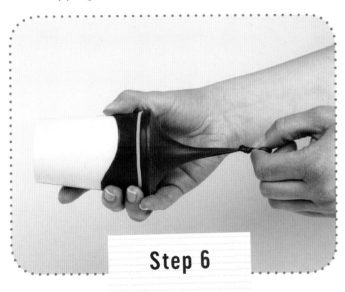

Step 6

To fire your air vortex cannon, pinch the tied knot of the stretched balloon, pull back gently, and release. Now you are ready to test how far air from your cannon can shoot.

Step 7

Tape a strip of toilet paper to a doorframe. Stand directly in front of the toilet paper and fire your cannon. Step back and fire again. Find the maximum distance from which air shooting from your cannon can travel while still exerting enough force to move the toilet paper. Measure and record the distance.

HOW DOES IT WORK?

Your air vortex cannon works by quickly applying force to air molecules inside the cup. When the balloon surface snaps forward, it collides directly with the air molecules inside the cup, forcing them out of the hole. When this fast-moving air shoots out of the cannon and mixes with the stationary air outside, it forms a vortex ring.

PAPER AIRPLANES

Investigate aerodynamics—the interaction between air and the objects moving through the air. Create and test three different paper airplane models. Which plane will fly farthest? Which will fly fastest? Which will fly straightest?

THE NEEDLE

This classic plane is built for speed—the harder you chuck it, the farther it goes.

Step 1

Using a ruler, draw the lines you see on a blank sheet of paper. Fold the paper in half on the center line, and open up the paper so it lies flat.

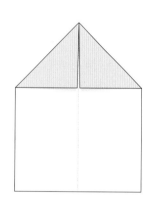

Step 2

Fold down both corners.

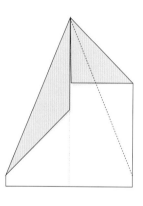

Step 3

Fold down the sides.

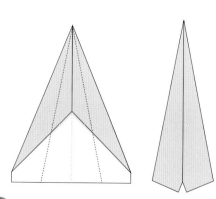

Step 4

Fold down the sides once more.

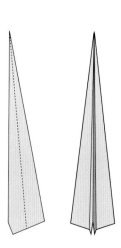

Step 5

Fold the plane in half along the center line. Then fold down each wing.

CLOUD DRAGON

This unusual design has a stabilizing forewing known as a canard.

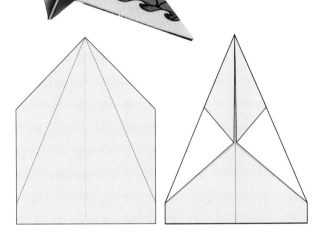

Step 1

Begin with a blank sheet of paper. Fold paper in half on center line, and open up paper so that it lies flat.

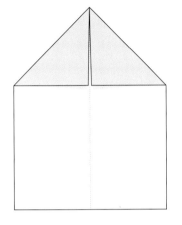

Step 2

Fold down both top corners.

Step 3

Turn plane over. Fold down both sides.

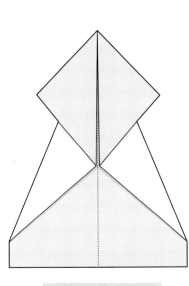

Step 4

Pull out flaps.

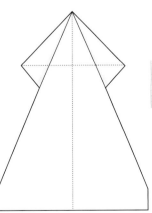

Step 5

Turn plane over. Fold down top.

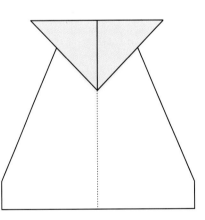

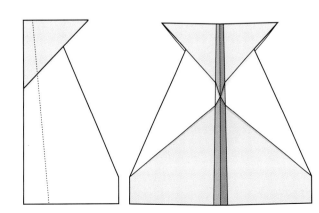

Step 6

Fold plane in half along the center line. Then fold down each wing.

57

BLUE YONDER

Blue Yonder is a glider that lives up to its name. With a good launch, this far-flying craft will go sailing into the blue!

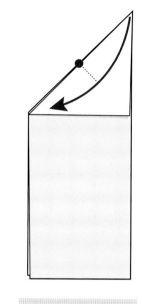

Step 1

Begin with a blank piece of paper. Fold paper in half (from left to right).

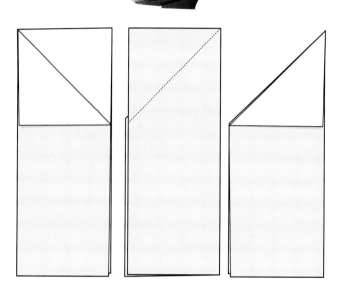

Step 2

Fold back each top corner.

Step 3

Fold the top point down to create a crease.

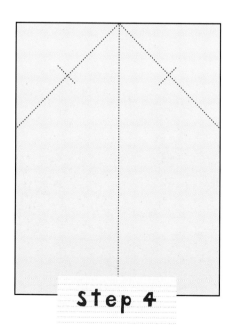

Step 4

Unfold paper and lay it flat.

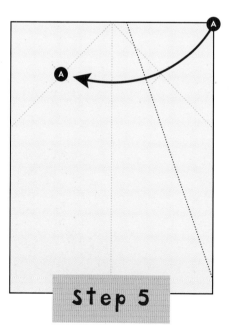

Step 5

Fold top corner to meet point A.

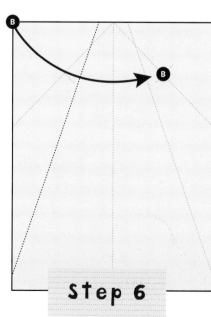

Step 6

Unfold. Repeat on the other side.

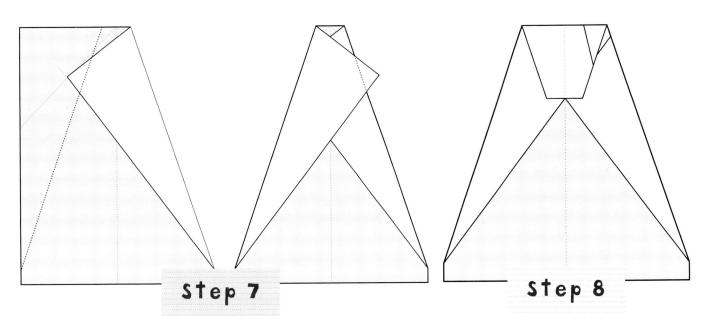

Step 7

Fold the two sides along the creases you just made. Fold and tuck the two points inward.

Step 8

Fold down the top.

Step 9

Fold the plane in half. Make sure you fold it so that the fold in step 8 is on the outside.

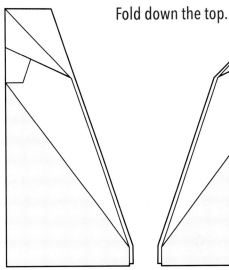

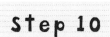 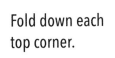

Step 10

Fold down each top corner.

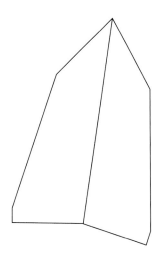

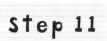 Fold down each wing.

NOW TRY THIS!

Fly all your planes. Which model stays in the air longest? Which model is fastest? The Needle speeds through the air because air passes around its streamlined shape easily without exerting much drag. Blue Yonder experiences lots of lift because its wings have a large area, allowing it to stay aloft longer.

PAPER ROCKETS

Make two paper rockets—one with fins and one without—
and test which is more stable.

MATERIALS

- Cardstock paper
- Two plastic straws
- Scissors
- Pencil
- Tape

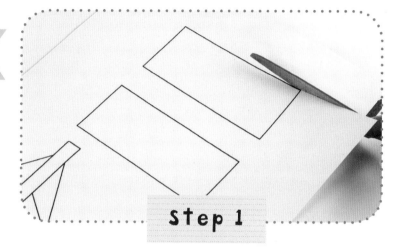

Step 1

Carefully cut out a 2" x 4 ½" rectangle. This will form the body tube of your rocket. Color or decorate, if desired.

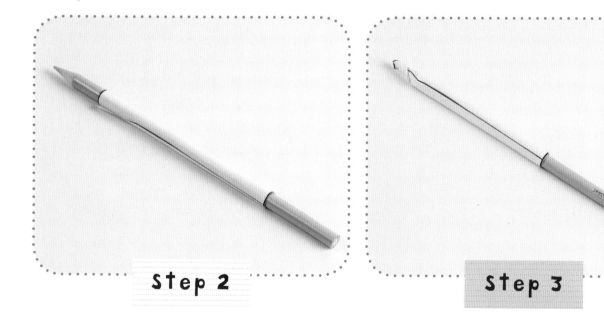

Step 2

Wrap the rectangle lengthwise around a pencil. Tape paper closed so that it forms a tube, but don't use tape at the very top end of the tube near the pencil tip.

Step 3

Twist the top of the body tube around the sharpened pencil tip, being careful not to rip the paper. This is the nose cone. Slide the rocket off the pencil. This completes the rocket without fins.

Step 4

Make another rocket following steps 1–3. This time you will add fins. Draw and cut out 2 fin units like the ones you see above.

Step 5

Each fin unit has 2 triangular fins separated by a narrow rectangle. Lay the first fin unit flat with outlines facing down. Place the body tube on top of the rectangle so the bottom of the rectangle aligns with the bottom of the body tube.

Step 6

Cut a piece of tape in half so you have 2 narrow pieces. Tape the fin unit to the body tube using one piece to wrap around the bottom of the rectangle and the other to wrap around the top of the rectangle.

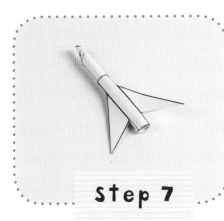

Step 7

Repeat steps 5–6 for the other fin unit, but tape it on the other side of the body tube. Both fin units should now be on opposite sides of the bottom of the rocket.

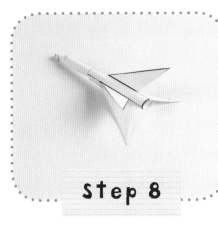

Step 8

Fold the fins up along the parallel lines on either side of the rectangle. The 4 fins should form a "+" shape, with each fin at a right angle (90 degrees) from its neighbor. This completes the rocket with fins.

Step 9

Compare the rockets. Slide each onto a straw and blow to launch. *Which rocket flies farther? Do the rockets fly straight or tumble in midair? Do fins make a rocket more stable?*

HOW DOES IT WORK?

The fins on your second rocket help keep it stable and pointed in the same direction. The rocket with fins should have flown straight and traveled farther as a result.

CRAFT STICK
CATAPULT

Catapults are simple machines that have been used since ancient times to hurl projectiles at enemies. Make your own catapult out of craft sticks and then test how far you can launch projectiles.

MATERIALS

- 8 jumbo craft sticks
- 5 rubber bands
- Bottle lid or cap
- Glue
- Pompoms or other soft projectiles
- Measuring tape or ruler

Step 1

Stack 6 jumbo craft sticks on top of each other. Secure the sticks together by tightly wrapping a rubber band around each end of the stack.

Step 2

Next, stack 2 craft sticks on top of each other. Secure tightly with a rubber band around just one end.

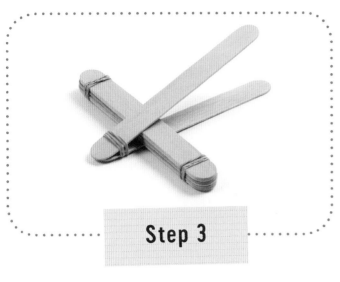

Step 3

Slide the stack of 6 sticks in between the unsecured end of the 2 sticks from step 2 as far as possible.

Step 4

Use 2 more rubber bands to secure both parts in place so that the rubber bands form an "X" where all the sticks meet.

Step 5

Add a dab of glue to the end of the launching arm that sticks up. Press the bottle lid down onto the glue. Hold firmly until glue is dry.

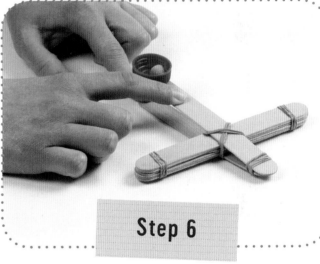

Step 6

To launch a projectile, place a pompom or other small object in the bottle lid. Hold the base of the catapult down with one hand. With the other hand, push the launching arm down and release! *How far can you launch your projectile? Measure with a ruler or measuring tape. What happens when you push the launching arm farther down?*

HOW DOES IT WORK?

Catapults work because energy can be converted from one type to another and transferred from one object to another. When you push down the launching arm, you add energy to it. This energy is stored as potential energy until you're ready to launch. When you let go, this stored energy is released and converted into kinetic energy—the energy of motion. The energy is transferred to the projectile (launched object), which then flies in the air.

NOTES

This book comes with a **free app** for your smartphone!
Download the **PI Learn to Code App*** from the **App Store** or **Google Play**.

Compatible Smartphones

The app was tested with the smartphones listed below. Other smartphones running Android 5.0 (Lollipop) or later OR iOS 9.0 or later may also be compatible. Google Nexus 5, Google Nexus 5X, Google Nexus 6, Motorola Moto Z, Apple iPhone 6, Apple iPhone 6 Plus, Apple iPhone 7, Apple iPhone 8, Apple iPhone X; Apple iPhone 11; Samsung Galaxy S6, Samsung Galaxy S6 Edge, Samsung Galaxy S7, Samsung Galaxy S8, Samsung Galaxy S9, Samsung Galaxy S10

App concept/design, interior/cover art, and photo styling by Lou Newton
Additional images from Shutterstock.com

Developed in partnership with Filament Games.

First printing
Manufactured in China.
03/2021 Guangdong
8 7 6 5 4 3 2 1

*We reserve the right to terminate the app.

**Smartphone not included. Standard data rates may apply to download. Once downloaded, the app does not use data or require Wi-Fi access.

Let's get social!

⃝ @Publications_International

🅕 @PublicationsInternational

🅕 @BrainGames.TM

www.pilbooks.com

CONTENTS

WHAT'S CODING?

First, most kinds of coding, including in our app, give you a set of tools that you use again and again. It's like a toolbox where you have a hammer and a screwdriver. Each of those tools is good for some kinds of jobs and not others.

So every time you need to hammer a nail, you use the hammer from your toolbox. But every time you use a hammer, some details change. Where are you using it? What kind of nail is it? Are you hammering it into a wall or a piece of furniture? The hammer is always the same, but you decide the rest of those things

Coding commands are the same way. When we use "Move," it's a single command. It doesn't tell you where, how fast, who's moving, or what direction they're moving. It does one thing. You wouldn't use a hammer to try to turn a screw, and you wouldn't use "Move" if you wanted your character to talk.

Second, it's okay to try things until you figure out what you want to happen. In our app, you'll use tools to make your characters move around and do things, by themselves or with other characters. It's easy to drag and drop the commands for each character and decide what you want them to do and say. But it's a little harder to think about what two characters will do together.

Don't worry if it seems hard! Thinking about how different objects work together is a challenge for programmers, too. Most of the time, they make plans that start long before they actually start to write code. They draw pictures and charts to show what they want their code to do. They think about how people will use their program.

You can do the same thing. What is your story? What are your characters doing? If you know a little bit about what you want a whole scene to be, you'll find it's easier to decide which commands to use. Just like a programmer, you'll almost never get it right the very first time. It's fun to experiment and play with commands to see what happens.

Finally, reading code is a lot like reading regular words. It's important to be able to look at a list of commands and figure out what the whole list is going to do. And just like a sentence, a list of commands should make sense. If your character is walking toward another character, it probably shouldn't stop in the middle or turn around and walk back to where it started.

Lists of commands are read top to bottom. Sometimes, for special commands like "Repeat," you can put a second list inside. Those inside lists follow the same rules. You read top to bottom, a certain number of times, and then continue reading the rest of your commands. "Move" then "Talk" does something different than "Talk" then "Move." If you make a list of commands and it isn't behaving like you think it should, think about the order.

HOME SCREEN

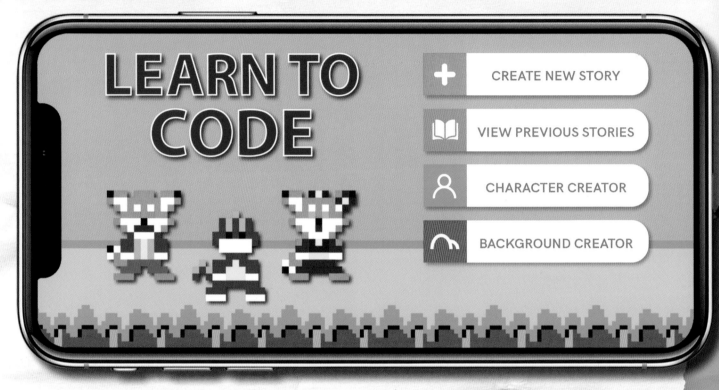

Finding your stories and characters is easy. From the main menu, you can get to everything. Here's what each button does.

 CREATE NEW STORY

When you press this button, you start a new story with blank pages where you can make characters and backgrounds or use the ones already in the app. With seven characters and seven backgrounds, you don't have to make anything unless you want to.

Give your story a title and start adding pages!

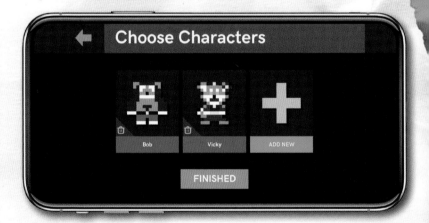

This is the first step of making a new story: picking the characters you want to include. You can choose preloaded characters, ones you already made by yourself, or make brand new characters by pressing the plus sign.

VIEW PREVIOUS STORIES

When you press this button, you see a list of stories you've worked on before. You can work on them again or play them for friends and family to watch.

Each story shows your title and which characters are in it. You can put a star on stories you want to go together – maybe they're your favorites, or maybe they're the ones you're still working on!

In your story library, you see each story's title and which characters are in it. It's easy to find the one you want!

CHARACTER CREATOR

When you press this button, you can go straight to the drawing! Make your own characters from scratch, or copy one of our seven fun characters. It's easy to change colors and add your own style. You can also see all the characters you've made before.

There are seven fun characters already in the app. Use them just as they are, make them look more like you or your friends, or add all new characters.

Add new characters by pressing the plus sign. Touch an existing character if you want to copy it – maybe your bear wears glasses or has a hat, or everybody has bright red shoes!

BACKGROUND CREATOR

Use the easy tile maker to make grass, sky, water – whatever you can dream up. Your tiles can even be animated if you want. Then use those tiles to make big scenes where your characters can walk and play and talk. They could have adventures in the ocean or on the Moon!

There are seven backgrounds already in the app. They have waves that splash, flowers that bloom, and plenty of room for your imagination.

DESIGNING CHARACTERS

To make characters, start with the Character Creator button.

Click the plus sign to add a new character.

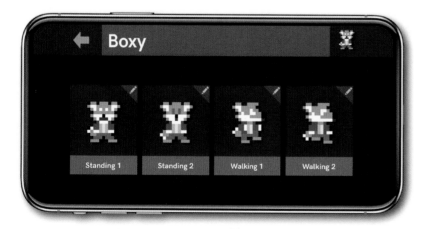

Your character only needs two views, front and side. When characters are hanging out and talking, they face front. When they're walking or running, they face the side. If it's hard to think about front and side views, look at these views of Boxy Fox.

We see different things from the front or the side, and animals or ghosts or aliens are the same way! Use your imagination to help you decide how your character looks from the side. If that's too hard, there's nothing wrong with having both character pictures face front! You can also ask your parents or teacher for help.

Tap on the **Front Facing Box** to get started.

USING THE PIXEL DRAWING SCREEN IS REALLY EASY!

HERE'S WHAT THE BUTTONS DO.

PENCIL TOOL

The pencil lets you color one pixel at a time, or hold and drag to keep drawing in a line or shape. If your phone has a stylus, you can use that! Otherwise, your finger works great.

PAINT CAN

The paint can lets you pick a color and fill a shape with that color. Characters usually aren't whole squares of color, so you'll use the paint can to fill in small areas like shirts. You can always color them in using the pencil, too! Any pixel squares you don't color with the pencil or paint can will be transparent, which means the background shows through

MOVE TOOL

Helps to move the design grid around to get a better view of where you are working while zoomed in.

CLEAR ALL

Clears all art from the design grid.

UNDO & REDO

If you draw a line you don't like or fill in the wrong area, press this button to undo it! But you can also redo, if you want that line after all.

ZOOM: IN & OUT

Allows you to zoom in and out to get a better view of your work.

ERASER TOOL

The eraser tool is the same as a pencil eraser. You can use it to erase one pixel square or the whole page. If you erase too much, you can undo it!

FRAME VIEW: BACKWARD / FORWARD

Allows you to see the different views that make up your animated tiles or characters.

COPY / PASTE

Use these tools to copy and paste an entire design to other frames.

FRONT FACING CHARACTERS

Think about your favorite books, games, and movies. The characters could be people like you or people different from you. They could be animals or plants that exist in real life. They could be household objects like toasters or sponges. They could be fantastical creatures or monsters! Let's design a character together using the Character Creator. We'll draw in individual pixels and make a simple version of our fox character just for practice. Later, you might want to make robots or sea creatures or space aliens or unicorns! Remember, any pixel squares you leave "blank" will be transparent, or see-through, so you don't have to fill in all the pixels.

1.

Think about what a fox looks like. If you aren't sure, ask someone to help you look it up in a book or online. A fox is a furry, orange animal that looks kind of like a dog and kind of like a cat. It has big pointy ears. Let's draw a round, orange head with pointy ears.

2.

We want to fit a head and a body for our character, but story characters don't have to look like anyone in real life. The head can be huge and the body can be really small! Let's plan to have a head that's 7 squares high and a body that's 6 squares high.

3.

A real fox has front and back legs and walks on all fours. Our fox is a pretend character and stands up like a person. Let's draw a simple body.

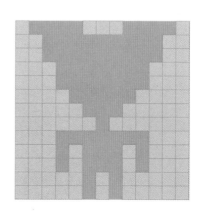

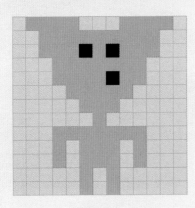

4.

Add dots for eyes, and a nose.

5.

A fox has a snout that sticks out of its face more than a person's nose.

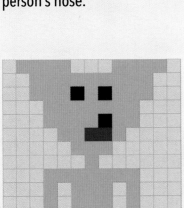

6.

Add just a couple of pixels to make the mouth. At this point, your fox could be finished! It's simple but lets you tell lots of stories.

7.

Let's add a few fun details, though. Foxes can have black ear tips and white ear fluff.

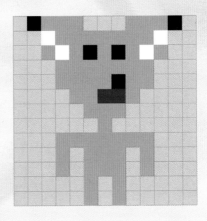

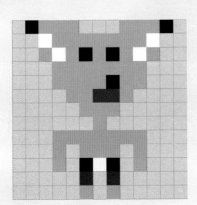

8.

Maybe our fox is wearing pants and a shirt! It's easy to turn real clothes into simple shapes for pixel drawing.

Finally, let's add a black belt with a yellow buckle.

SIDE FACING CHARACTERS

In ancient Egypt, people drew and painted murals. They made such sturdy buildings that we still have some of this art even though it's thousands of years old! And they liked to draw people facing sideways, but do you notice anything strange? Look close and think about it. Did you notice that the eyes look like they're facing forward?

In real life, our eyes look more like triangles when we face sideways. Why did the Egyptians decide to draw them a different way? We can guess some reasons. The Egyptians really liked how eyes looked – they used eyes in their hieroglyphics, or picture language, and they used heavy black makeup to draw around their eyes to make them look bigger and more important. Drawing eyes this way definitely gives their art a special style that is easy to notice right away.

When you're drawing with pixels, you don't have to worry about your characters looking just like real life. It's fun to play and try different things to see what you like. We're drawing characters that will walk and talk, so you probably want to draw them differently for front and side views. That doesn't mean you have to study and do perfect side views!

1.

Let's draw a side view of our simple fox from before. Like with our front view, we want to fit a bigger head and a smaller body. Let's plan to have a head that's 7 squares high and a body that's 6 squares high.

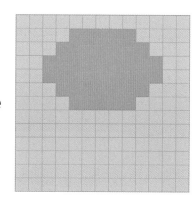

2.

Think about what a fox looks like. If you aren't sure, ask someone to help you look it up in a book or online. A fox is a furry, orange animal that looks kind of like a dog and kind of like a cat. It has big pointy ears. Do you have a dog or know someone who has a dog? From the side, a fox looks a lot like a dog. Let's draw an oval for a head. We need room for a long nose, so don't draw the head right in the middle! Move it a little bit to the side.

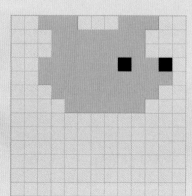

3.

Add pointy ears to the top of the head. Draw a nose by adding pixels on the right side. Our character is already starting to look like a fox!

4.

Draw a simple black pixel dot for an eye. Since our fox is facing sideways, there's just one eye in this view!

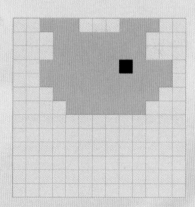

5.

Add a black dot at the tip of the nose.

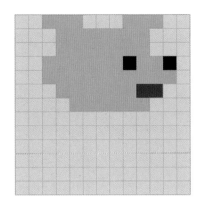

6.

Use a couple of red pixels to draw the mouth. Our fox looks a lot more "real" in the side view! Why is that? Well, people and foxes have faces with parts that stick out, and it's really hard to draw "sticking out" noses and other face parts in our simple pixel grid. This is a big challenge! From the side, these shapes are easier to draw.

But that's not true for everything. A flower might look pretty flat from the side, but be round and bright and complicated when you look at it from the front! You could make a flower character and work it out.

7.

Now, we'll add the same simple kind of body we used before.

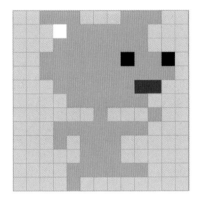

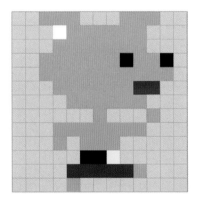

8.

And finally, some clothes!

Our fox has a front view and a side view, so we're ready to move on to the next step.

Sometimes, it's easy to follow directions that go step by step, but then it feels much harder to draw your own characters. If you feel confused or aren't sure, think about your favorite cartoon characters. Ask someone to help you look up pictures of those characters, and see how your favorite artists made their characters look different from the front or the side. Every artist has to decide how to make their characters look how they want! There's not just one "right" way to draw – you're the artist and you get to decide.

Once your characters have a front view and a side view, they're ready to go into your stories. But you can add a second frame, which means your character can blink, wiggle, wag its tail, or anything else you can dream up. What if you were a character? For a person who is walking forward, you could do one frame with their left leg up and one with their right leg up. Maybe your character is waving, so the second frame has their hand moving to show the wave. Maybe your character is a robot and the second frame has all its light-up buttons turned on. Maybe your character is a color-changing chameleon and the second frame is the same animal with bright polka dots!

The characters that are already in the app are mostly animals, and their second frames are fun and simple. Let's look at some of them to help you get more ideas! In each case, the character is almost exactly the same with just a few pixels that change to show that it's moving.

Frame: a frame is one step of an animation. In a cartoon, each tiny movement is a new frame of animation!

The fox wags its tail and blinks. In the side view, it looks up and down and its feet move up and down. What else could you do with this fox character? it could open and close its mouth. Its ears could wiggle. If you drew a fox that was holding a magic wand, it could wave the wand or the wand could light up!

The bear closes and opens its eyes and mouth. In the side view, its feet move up and down and it moves its eyes. What else could the bear do? It could open its mouth wide like a roar in the front view and tilt its head back in the side view.

The gator blinks and bares its teeth and its tail wiggles. In the side view, its feet move up and down, it bares its teeth, and it wiggles its tail. What if you changed its ridge of light-green spikes so they changed colors from frame to frame? What if it breathed fire?

The octopus closes and opens its eyes and waves its tentacles. What else could it do? The octopus could float up and down, like it would in the ocean. Its tentacles could pull in and float back out. It could even tilt to one side. It's fun to have an ocean animal who can move all around without gravity!

The bird opens and closes its beak and flaps its wings. What else could the bird do? Maybe you want the bird to carry something that it could hold in its claws. It could have a feather crest that moves up and down. The bird could tilt back and forth or move up and down as it flies.

PLANES, TRAINS, & AUTOMOBILES

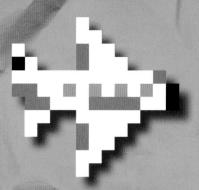

For a very long time, people have used all kinds of things to carry them around. Even before someone invented the round wheel, people put their stuff on sleds that they pulled around. In ancient Egypt, they used smooth logs from trees to help them roll heavy rocks!

Anything that moves people or stuff around, like a car or a sled, is called a vehicle. And your stories could include all kinds of vehicles as characters! Remember that a character doesn't have to talk – you might make a truck because your fox character is a truck driver. But a talking car could be fun! Even before Pixar started making *Cars* movies, real-life cars have played helpers and sidekicks.

Here are a few characters you could make and use in your stories.

This helicopter is like ones that the U.S. military has used since the 1950s. It has a big bubble front with a really lightweight tail. What kinds of characters could fly in a helicopter? What kinds of stories could you tell about them?

Your characters could ride in a small car or a school bus. Since the car is puffing out exhaust, it could make a windy sound as it drives around. The car has plain blue windows but the school bus has transparent windows – remember, transparent means you can see through to what's behind it. That could be really cool if your characters are going on a vacation or field trip!

Our examples don't look like real-life cars or helicopters. But when you look at them, you can tell what they are, just like in cartoons. How could you turn some of these different vehicles into pixel characters for your stories?

DESIGNING BACKGROUNDS

To make backgrounds, start with the Background Creator button.

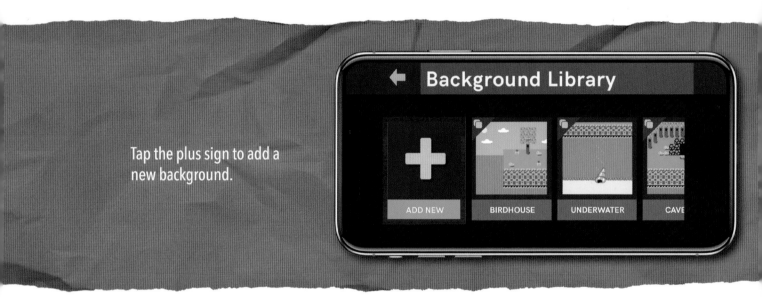

Tap the plus sign to add a new background.

Drawing backgrounds may look a lot like drawing characters, but there are a few big changes between the two! Backgrounds are made of individual squares called tiles. You draw tiles the same way you draw characters, one pixel at a time.

First, we draw tiles one at a time, but we use one tile over and over. You can even use the paint can tool to fill spaces with tiles like you would with solid colors.

Second, our characters can be any shape, but background tiles are all square. We need to plan to fill those squares all the way up!

Third, our characters are just one "tile" worth of pixels, but we can draw huge shapes if we use tiles put together, like a whale or dinosaur or a huge mountain.

Finally, tiles can have up to three frames total. Remember, a frame is a part of an animation. Characters have two frames so they can blink or walk. Tiles have up to three frames, which means they can move more.

Tap on the
Blank Background
to get started.

USING THE TILE DRAWING
SCREEN IS REALLY EASY!

HERE'S WHAT THE BUTTONS DO.

 PENCIL TOOL

The pencil lets you color one tile at a time, or hold and drag to keep drawing in a line or shape. If your phone has a stylus, you can use that! Otherwise, your finger works great.

 PAINT CAN

The paint can lets you pick a tile and fill a shape with that color.

 MOVE TOOL

Helps to move the design grid around to get a better view of where you are working while zoomed in.

 BACKGROUND COLOR FILL

Fills the entire background with color.

 CLEAR ALL

Clears all art from the design grid.

 **UNDO & REDO**

Undo or redo last step.

 **ZOOM: IN & OUT**

Allows you to zoom in and out to get a better view of your work.

 ERASER TOOL

The eraser tool is the same as a pencil eraser. You can use it to erase one pixel square or the whole page. If you erase too much, you can undo it!

 **TILE EDIT TOOLS**

Add a new blank tile. Edit a selected tile. Delete selected tile.

 **COPY / PASTE**

Use these tools to copy and past an entire design to other frames.

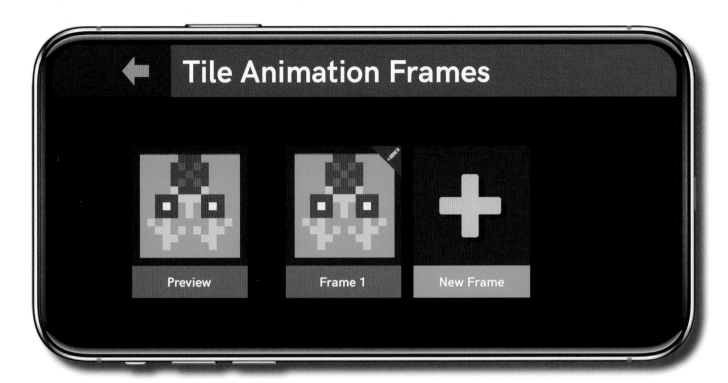

Preview   Frame 1   New Frame

How do you start making backgrounds? It's different than making characters, but it's still easy to do.

1. When you click Background Creator on the home screen, you'll go to your Background Library. Click the plus sign on the left to add a new background. You'll see a blank new background show up right next to the plus sign. Click the pencil icon on the top right.

2. Now we're looking at the whole blank background. You can give it a name if you want! And if you really don't want to draw any tiles, you can fill the whole background with solid color using the diamond button on the left side.

3. To start making tiles, press the plus sign on the right side of the blank background. Then press the pencil button under it to edit your new tile.

4. The Tile Animation Frames screen shows a preview of your tile. Every tile has one frame automatically, and you can click the pencil icon in the top right corner to draw your first frame.

★ That's all you need to get started. In the rest of this section, we'll show you different ways to design backgrounds and turn your ideas into reality!

DESIGNING TILES

Now that we know about the character maker and the tools in the background maker, we can start to make tiles. Think of a tile as a paintbrush that you'll use to "paint" onto your whole backgrounds. So if you want a sidewalk, you can draw a sidewalk tile once and then use it as many times as you want! This is how a lot of games are made. It saves a lot of time!

Is there a tile floor somewhere in your home or school? One tile by itself is blue or brown or any other color. When you have a bunch of tiles all together, the whole floor looks blue or brown or whatever color. Each tile we make will be put next to a lot of other tiles to make a "floor" of grass, hot lava, pavement, a sandy beach – anything you can dream up.

For now, we'll make tiles that are flat, meaning they don't have a second frame. But we'll talk about making animated tiles later in the book! Let's learn the basics first. We'll start with making a grass tile for a simple scene with grass and sky.

With each step, we'll make our grass tile look more like real grass. It will never look all the way real, and we don't need anything to look perfect! Think about how you want your background to look, and don't stress about details – it should be fun. We'll go through some different ways to think about how to draw grass. Try the ones you want, mix different kinds together, whatever feels like the best way to tell your stories.

SHADED GRASS

We can use dots of color to make different "shades" of green grass to use in our backgrounds.

1. The very easiest way to make grass is just to color the whole tile green. That will look fine in your backgrounds! Let's color our tile all green with the paint-can tool.

2. Next, we'll make a green tile with a few dots of lighter green.

3. We can add even more light dots, and then even more! Here's how those will look as tiles.

4. Eventually, our grass tile will have enough light dots that it looks like a different color when it's all tiled together.

5. We'll start by coloring a tile with light green and add dark green as the dots! We've flipped from when we started with dark green and dots of light green.

6. For our seventh and eighth tiles, we'll use fewer and fewer dark green dots on our light green tiles.

We're using these steps to make grass tiles, and now we have a full set of eight that we can use to make all kinds of backgrounds. What if your characters were exploring a tall hill? What if they were taking a diagonal path?

You can use the same idea, where you add more and more dots of color, to make all kinds of different backgrounds. If your dots were of tan and orange, your tiles could be the desert. If they were blue, they could be the ocean. Instead of green, what if you used black and purple?

Now our grassy path is a galaxy in a beautiful sky at night, or the stage for a famous singer—there's no limit to your imagination.

SWIRLING GRASS

Let's try another way to draw grass with tiles. Afterward, we'll see how many other kinds of backgrounds we can draw using the same idea – not just grass! But we'll start with a whole green tile again. Then we'll draw swirls that will go all the way across our whole background. It's easy when you know a helpful trick.

1. Think about how our tiles fit together. They always go in a big square, so if you draw a line across your tile, it will go all the way across your whole background! Let's draw a light green line straight across our tile.

And see how it looks when some tiles are put together?

2. Let's add a few more lines that go across our tile.

Now our grid of tiles has stripes we can use as a guide when we draw swirls.

3. It's time for our trick! We use dark green to "erase" most of each line we just drew, but leave one pixel on each end. These guide pixels will make sure our tiles connect right when we put a bunch of them together.

4. Now we can draw swirling lines between each set of dots.

See how these tiles, put together, create one long swirl that goes all the way across?

5. We can even connect dots that aren't right across from each other. Look at this tile where straight lines connect different dots.

But even a mix of both kinds of tiles makes nice swirling lines that go all the way across! Any tile we make with the same trick will fit together this way. This one looks like a braid!

6. We can add a few dots of white to our braid tile to make tiny white flowers or snowflakes.

Using a few of these tiles on our grassy area makes it look even better.

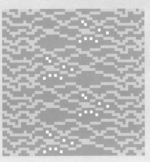

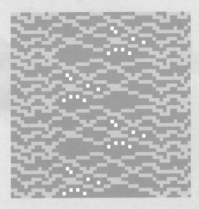

How would our swirl design look with different colors? We can use it to make almost anything.

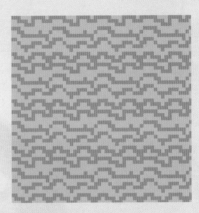

If we use blue, it looks like the ocean.

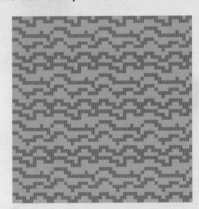

If we use orange, it looks like hot lava!

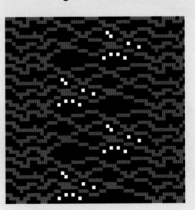

Even our meadow of flowers turns into a spooky cave, with animal eyes peeking out.

USING THE TILE LIBRARY

Think about drawing with markers. You have some colors to use, and you have something you want to draw. When you think of ideas to draw, you don't only think in the colors of markers you have. Our imaginations have millions of colors! But you pick the closest color of marker and do your best, and your picture turns out great.

In the Background Creator, you have a tile library instead of a color palette. You'll click the plus sign to add a new tile, then click the edit button to draw the tile. We've talked about some cool ways to draw tiles, and you'll put those tiles together in your tile library. You can pick tiles and draw with them onto your backgrounds, like you would with markers and paper.

How many tiles do you need to make a background? You don't need to draw any if you don't want to draw them. With the diamond-shaped button in the app, you can fill the background in with any of our colors. Maybe your characters are birds who fly in the sky for the whole story, or little spaceships that fly in plain black space.

It's easy to use just one kind of tile, too. Space can be plain black or you can add a few white dots for stars. A sky could be all blue with just a few puffy white clouds.

But you can use as many different kinds of tiles as you want, too. The backgrounds that we put in the app for you to use have around 8 different tiles each. Here's a whole background we made with the tiles we've drawn so far in this book. Our three talking trees are hanging out on a beach with other characters. There are only 8 kinds of tiles in this scene. If we didn't want to add trees and a squirrel for fun, we'd only need 4 different tiles!

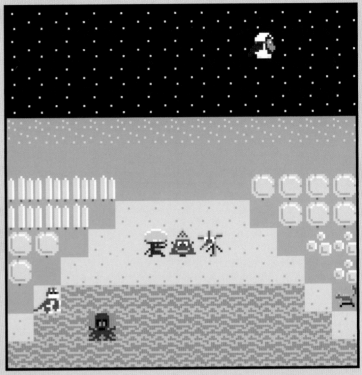

If we wanted to make a smoother edge on our beach, we could add some tiles that have two different colors on a diagonal. This new scene has just 4 more tiles to make the smoother edges.

You can always keep adding more details and doing more coloring to make your tiles look more like you see them in your imagination.

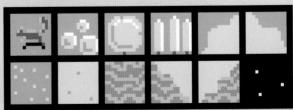

SECOND FRAMES

We have added blinks and other small animations to our characters. You can add these little changes to your background tiles, too!

We've drawn a lot of background tiles together already – let's look at some of these tiles and add some action by using extra frames. Each set of frames is one complete tile that will wiggle, bloom, or some other action.

The left frame shows white flowers on a section of simple green grass. On the right, we redrew the flowers so they'll look like they're moving and twirling a little bit.

A nice round tree on the left is just shortened a little in the frame on the right. When the frames switch back and forth, it will bop up and down.

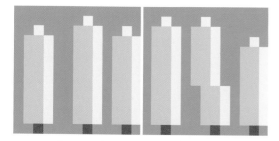

On the left are three tall skinny trees. The left-most tree will move up and down. The middle tree will wave back and forth. The right-most tree will also move up and down.

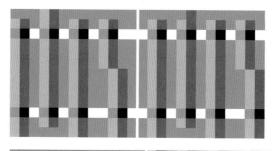

A rickety beach fence waves back and forth in these two frames. All the art is just moved over one square!

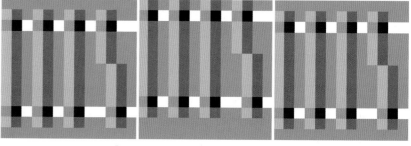

Here, our beach fence is a rickety bridge, and we added two frames to make it sway in the wind. Imagine waiting to cross a bridge that was swinging back and forth – this is an easy way to add a scary mood in your story!

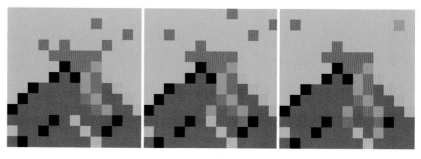

On the left is the original volcano, and in the two extra frames, the lava flies further into the air and drips down the side of the volcano.

TRANSPARENCY

When we designed and drew our characters, we left blank space so the background would show through. That makes sense – people, animals, trees, and space creatures are all different shapes, not just squares.

But we can use transparent, or see-through, tiles for our backgrounds too. Now that you've practiced making tiles and backgrounds and giving them some "wiggle room" with extra frames, we can learn about transparency.

Using the diamond tool in the background creator, you can turn the whole background one color. What that means is that from frame to frame, you only have to change the other colors. If the sky is blue, you only have to draw the white clouds or the yellow sun. If the grass is green, you only have to draw light green for little details, colorful flowers, brown tree trunks, or whatever else is in your background.

Let's look at a bunch of the tiles we've made so far plus some new ones. You can see the whole tile with a background color in the top row. In the bottom row, there is no background color.

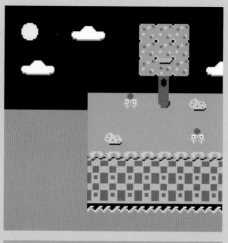
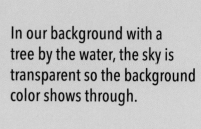
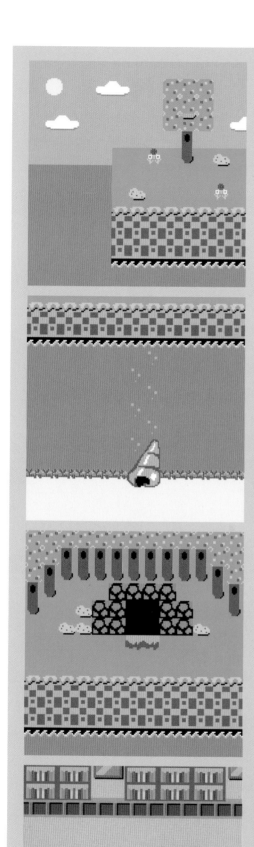
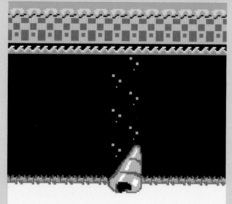

In our background with a tree by the water, the sky is transparent so the background color shows through.

Our seashell house at the bottom of the ocean has a transparent water background.

The rocky cave only has a little bit of transparency, but you could color the whole background green. Then you wouldn't have to draw all the green tiles.

The inside of our house has a transparent wall – it'll be easy to redecorate!

CREATING A STORY

From the home screen, click Create New Story.

Press the plus sign to add a character — you have to add at least one!

When you've added all the characters you want (up to four), press Finished.

Now you're on the screen where you add scenes. Click on New Story at the top of the screen to give your new story a title.

A scene starts with a background, then you add your characters and tell them what to do. Press the plus sign to add your first scene.

You'll see a blank white square where you can press the pencil icon in the top right corner to start making your scene.

You can choose from all the backgrounds that come with the app, plus any you've already made. Touch the one you want to use.

Now your scene has a background. In the next screen, you can see the whole background and all the characters you can use in your story.

Touch and drag each character to where you want them on the background.

Press the edit button below a character to get to the coding screen for that character.

COMMANDS

What are the commands in the app, and what do they do? Let's learn them all real quick in the next few pages, then we'll give more examples and ideas for each command later in the book.

In the Do Action section, your characters move, talk, and more.

 **Visible**

Your character can turn invisible or turn "un-invisible" again. They might be playing hide and seek and disappear behind a tree. They might be a warlock who appears suddenly!

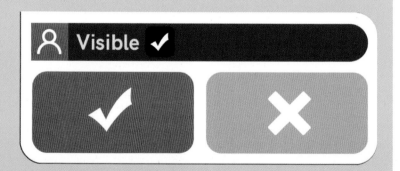

▶▶ Move

Characters can move up, down, left, or right. They can move at different speeds, too. If you want your character to walk a few steps left then a few steps down, that will be two different Move blocks: one for moving left, then a second one for moving down.

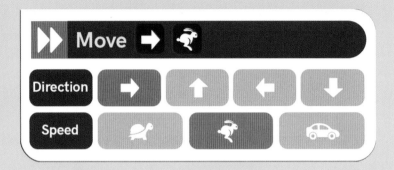

💬 Say

You decide what each character says and how long the speech bubble stays on the screen. It takes longer to read more words!

❗ Emote

You may not know the word "emote," but it's the same as emotions or emojis. Your characters can show that they're feeling four different feelings like happy and sad. An emoji floats over the character, and you decide how long it stays there.

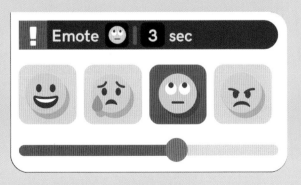

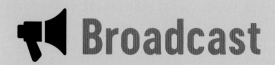 Broadcast

This command is like a relay race, where one character passes the baton to the next character you want to move or talk.

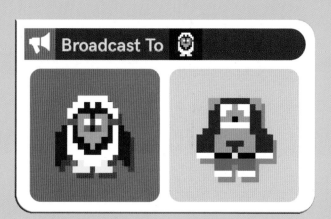

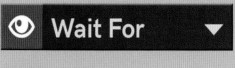 Wait For ▼

 Wait

You can choose for characters to stand still or stay invisible until a few seconds have passed.

 Broadcast

This is also where you send Broadcast commands — the waiting character will receive the signal!

 # Play Sound

Use this command to add a sound effect to your scene.

Play Fun Laugh				
SFX	Balloon	Bark	Beep 1	Beep 2
Bird Song	Boing 1	Boing 2	Boom 1	Boom 2
Bubbling	Chirp	Chord Happy	Chord Sad	Crickets
Doorbell	Footsteps 1	Footstep 2	Frog Croak	Ghost
Horse	Knock	Evil Laugh	Fun Laugh	Meow
Surprise	Pew Pew	Rain	Ripping	Roar
Trombone	Splash	Squeak	Thunder	Glass
Water Drip	Whistle	Whomp	Wind	Zap

Repeat

Instead of using 10 different Move commands, you can put one Move command inside a Repeat and make it play 10 times. The Repeat can hold as many commands as you want, and it will do all of them in order each time.

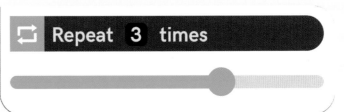

Repeat **3** times

MOVE

Let's talk about the Move command.

Remember how our characters have two "facing forward" frames and two "facing sideways" frames? These frames switch back and forth to make the characters more interesting to look at. When your characters act out the Move command, they'll use the "facing sideways" frames.

After you drag a Move command into your story, it has an arrow pointing to the right and a picture of a turtle on it. These are the default settings. Touch the arrow or the turtle to open the Move options.

A default is the way something automatically is, unless you decide to change it. Your phone or tablet has a default picture as its background before you choose your own wallpaper.

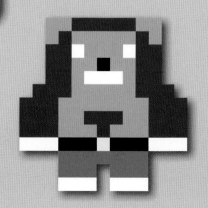

36

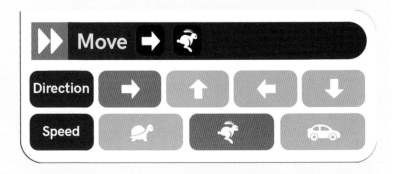

The arrow shows which direction your character is moving in: up, down, left, or right. Touch a different arrow to change the direction.

The turtle shows how fast your character will move. Choose the rabbit to move at a middle speed, and choose the car to move fast. Your character will move one square per Move block, no matter what speed you choose. It will just take a longer time for a slower speed, or a shorter time for a faster speed.

If you want characters to move in different directions, you can put two, three, or more Move blocks back to back. Try this and see what happens. If you want a character to move from bottom left to top right, the character needs to move right and up, but there are different ways to do that. You could alternate one square right and one square up until the character is all the way there. Or you could move all the way right and then, afterward, all the way up.

How can speeds affect your story?

You might want characters to run away from each other or from a monster. But you can use slow speeds to show that a character is thinking hard about something. What if an octopus invites their friend to swim, but the friend isn't sure? The friend might slowly walk up to the edge of the water. A friend who's excited to swim will probably run in!

SAY

Some of the best stuff people have ever made — including movies and TV, but also books, games, and even music — is about talking. What people say to each other is really important! So it's cool to think about what your characters can say in your stories.

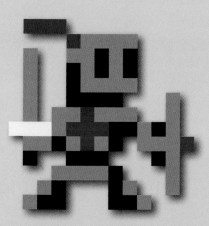

When you hold and drag a Say command into your story, it will show a blank rectangle and the number 3. Press either of those to open up the place to type in your words.

Each Say block can hold up to 50 letters, numbers, spaces, or whatever else you want characters to "say" in a speech bubble. Anything in your phone's keyboard is fair game, including symbols. If you reach the limit, you won't be able to type any more things into the window, so don't worry about typing something that gets cut off.

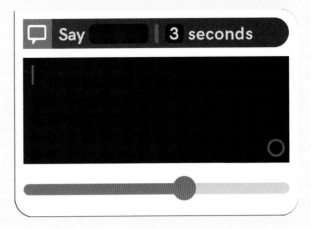

The number 3 in this screen shows how many seconds the speech bubble will stay visible in your story. It's set to 3 by default, but you can use the slider to change it to anything from 1 to 10 seconds. Remember: everybody is different, and some of us read slower or faster than other people. It's better to have too much time to read than not enough time!

Could you tell a whole story where characters stood in one place and just talked? This would be tough, but it could be fun to try! With friends or family, we almost have one long conversation that just starts and stops when we get to see each other or talk on the phone or chat. We don't say our names again every time we eat lunch with friends.

In your story, how will your characters say who they are, without sounding weird? Maybe your idea includes that they're meeting for the first time.

Have you seen a movie or cartoon of the story *A Christmas Carol*? In that story, a grouchy old man and a ghost watch different things happen. The ghost uses magic to move them from place to place. Your characters could stand still while the background changes around them. They could talk together for so long that it goes from day to night and gets dark!

Sometimes, TV shows make episodes where characters spend the whole episode in the same place. These are called "bottle episodes" because the characters are like ships in a bottle and can't just go wherever they want.

WAIT

Move and Say are both pretty easy to understand. Every day, we move around! We say things. You might think "Wait" is something more difficult, but we just don't think about how much time we spend waiting in a lot of different kinds of situations. Your characters will need to wait sometimes too.

A few pages ago, we talked about using speed to show how a character might be feeling, like moving slowly to do something they might not want to do. Using Wait can also be a good way to show that a character is thinking or feeling unsure. You can use it to keep one character out of your main action until you're ready for them to walk into the scene. You can use it to show that your character knows something will happen and they're being patient.

You can even use Wait to show that a character is getting bored because nothing is happening. In video games, characters often have special animations they do when you don't use the controller to move them for a few seconds. These are called idle animations and they're usually funny. One of the most common ones is for your character to go to sleep until you move the controller again.

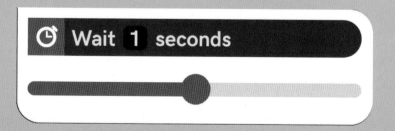

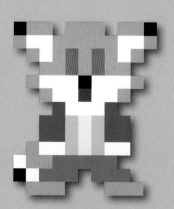

But Wait is even more useful than that. Think about what happens when you talk with someone. You say something, and then they say something, and you go back and forth. While you're not talking, you're listening . . . and waiting!

Let's look at how time works when you're having a conversation.

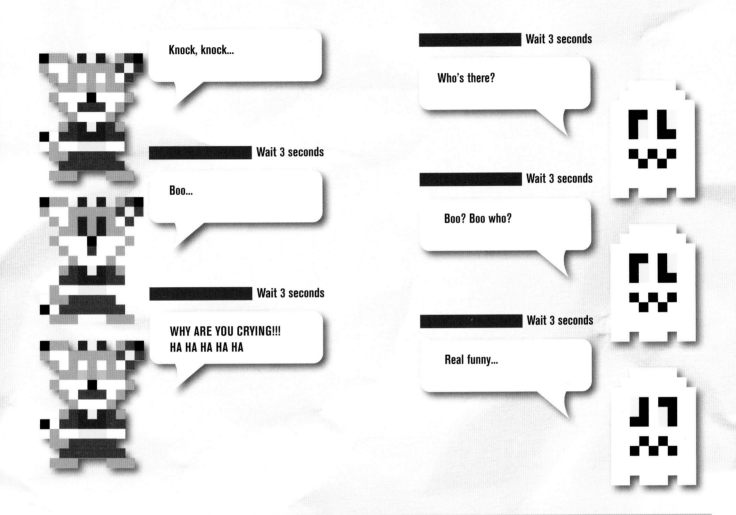

So someone coding YOU, if you were a story, would include just as many Wait blocks as Say blocks during this conversation. And the person you're talking to would be the mirror image, using Wait while you're doing Say, and doing Say while you're using Wait.

Programmers use a bunch of different kinds of waiting. Keeping track of time, in general, is a really important part of coding. Companies and offices have things they do every day at certain times. Computers can be taught to run a program or do a job at a specific time. Just like you know you get to eat lunch at 11:30 or go outside to recess at 9:45, computers can learn they do some things each day at the same times. We'll talk more about that later in the book.

LET'S TAKE A SWIM

Now that we know Move, Say, and Wait for Time, we can start making stories. We'll start with a really simple story about one character, using three backgrounds that come with the app. The alligator character will take a swim from its log home in the swamp, through the deep water, and ending up in the water by a tall cliff.

Start a new story, then add the alligator character from the app. That's all we'll need this time. In the screen where you add scenes, add the background with a log in a swamp, the totally underwater one, and the tree on a cliff overlooking the water.

Press Edit in the top right corner on the scene with the log in a swamp. You'll see the background art on the left side with your characters — just the alligator, this time — in a panel on the right.

Press and drag the alligator into the scene. It can start wherever you want, but for our story, we'll put it in the water near the log as a good starting place.

Once the alligator is in place, press the "piece of paper" button below the alligator icon in the character panel. Now we're in the place where you drag and drop commands to tell the character what to do.

We're just practicing our commands, so let's have the alligator say something. Touch and drag a Say block over into the left side, under the Start On Play block, then press on the blank space in the block to bring up the menu. Touch the place where the text will go, and type in whatever you want. In our example, we'll have the alligator say, "Where is everybody?" We can leave the default three-second time.

Since the alligator is looking for its friends, let's have it wait a few seconds. Drag a Wait For Time block so it sits below the Say block. Touch the number box in the Wait block and use the slider to choose how much time you want.

After asking and waiting, the alligator is going to swim through the neighborhood to look for its friends. Drag a Move block and drop it below the Wait block. Touch the arrow in the Move block to bring up the Move menu. Wherever you've put your alligator, it will need to make its way to the top of the swamp, without swimming "through" the log. How can you move the alligator so it stays in only the blue spaces of water? You might have to guess and check. We want the alligator to end up in a blue spot along the top of the water.

So you choose the direction that's right for your story, and the speed doesn't matter. If your alligator is more than one tile space away, drag a second Move block, and keep doing that until you have enough Moves to get the alligator to the top of the water.

Now we're ready for the alligator to swim out into the deep open water!

Press the arrow in the top left to go back to the Scenes screen.

Click the Edit button on the next scene -- the deep water with the seashell house. We'll have our alligator swim through, stop to check if its friend is at home in the seashell, then keep swimming.

Drag and drop the alligator toward the bottom of the left side of the scene. It needs to swim toward the seashell house, and we'll use Move blocks to get there. Press and drag five Move blocks in a row. It's easier to line them all up and then change the speed or direction if you want.

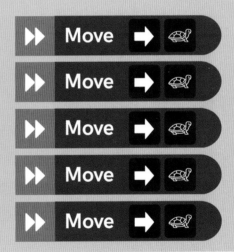

The alligator will stop and call out for his friend. Drag a Say block over to your command list, then have the alligator say something like "Is anybody here?"

Use more Move blocks to bring the alligator all the way over to the right side of the scene. There will be a bunch of Move blocks!

If you want, you can have the alligator pause again using a Wait For Time block. Try dragging a Wait block to somewhere in between your Move blocks. They move out of the way and make a space for the block you want to drop in.

Back out of the seashell-house scene and touch the Edit button on the cliffside scene.

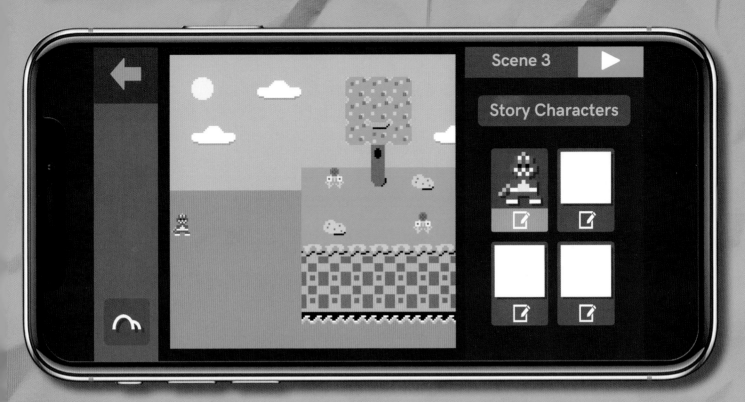

How should our quick story end? The alligator won't find his friends in this story, so that can't be our happy ending.

First, drag the alligator to the left side of the scene, somewhere toward the top of the blue water. Press the Edit button under the alligator in the panel to add commands.

Use a few Move blocks to make the alligator swim right, toward the cliff. Then use a Say block to have the alligator call out one more time: "Where are my friends?"

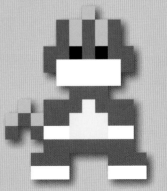

We're going to have the alligator pause and then say something funny to finish the story. But what should we have it say? The best jokes have surprises. What would be a really surprising thing for the alligator to say to finish our story?

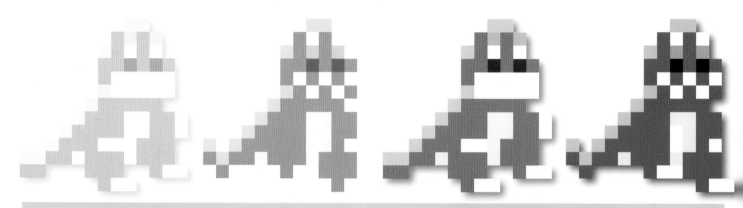

Drag a Wait For Time block, a Say block, a Play Sound block, and one last Say block into the command list. In the first Say block, type just "Oh…" For the Play Sound, choose the Evil Laugh sound. And in the last Say block, type "They're in my belly!"

BEAR WITH ME

Let's tell another simple story to practice our commands. This time, we'll use just one scene, but add a second character. We'll have to think about how they're acting at the same time, waiting for each other to talk, and more things about timing.

From the home screen, touch Create New Story and add two characters. We'll use the fox and the bear for our example. In the next screen, choose the background with the stony cave.

What kind of story can we tell with two characters who are moving around and talking? This background has lots of different kinds of things — bushes, trees, a cliff over the water, and the outside and inside of the cave. It could be fun to have the bear lose its house keys (or cave keys!) somewhere in the area and look in different places.

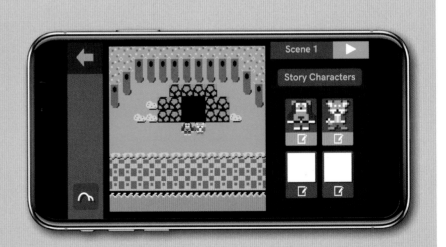

Press the Edit button on the cave scene, then drag the fox and the bear into the scene. Let's put them both on the brown path outside the cave.

Click the Edit button under the bear. Drag these blocks into place:

Move ← 🐢

Move ← 🐢

Move ← 🐢

Move ↑ 🐢

Wait 2 sec

Say I can't ... | 3 sec   Say: "I can't find my keys!"

Move ↑ 🐢

Wait 2 sec

Say They ... | 3 sec   Say: "They were here a minute ago! Oh...wait..."

Move ↓ 🚗

Move ↓ 🚗

Move → 🚗

Move → 🚗

Move → 🚗

Move ↑ 🚗

Say They'r... | 3 sec   Say: "They're on the table."

Wait 1 sec

Say Sorry!!... | 3 sec   Say: "Sorry!!"

That's all for the bear. Press the fox at the top to switch to the fox's commands. Drag these blocks into place:

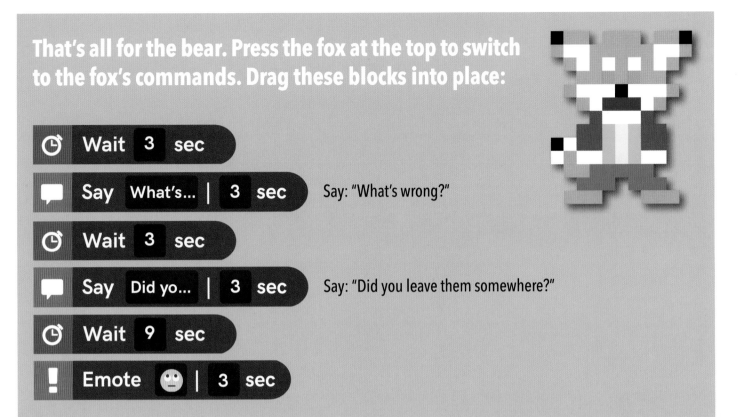

🕐 Wait **3** sec

💬 Say **What's... |** **3** sec Say: "What's wrong?"

🕐 Wait **3** sec

💬 Say **Did yo... |** **3** sec Say: "Did you leave them somewhere?"

🕐 Wait **9** sec

❗ Emote 😐 **|** **3** sec

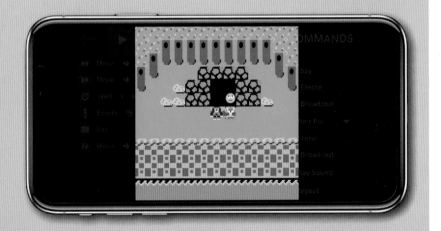

Press the Play button and watch how this scene unfolds. The bear walks around and looks for the keys while the fox waits, patiently at first, and then less patiently. There are a lot of moving parts that need to go back and forth between the fox and the bear for this scene to work right.

Go back into your command list for the bear, and change around some of the parameters. Remember, you can change them back by referring to the list on this page, so you won't break anything. But change the numbers in the Wait blocks, or change the speeds in the Move block from turtle to car or vice versa. Then run the story again and see what happens.

When the speeds and numbers change, all the parts of your story get jumbled. Timing everything is really important. We've given you an example that's already balanced, but try making your own story using the fox and the bear. Think about the time spent talking and waiting and how those two ideas have to go together for your story to work.

RACE TO THE FINISH

For our third sample story, we're going to bring in a new idea that we'll learn in more detail in the next few pages. It's the Repeat block.

In our first two stories, we ended up using a lot of Move blocks in a row. To take characters all the way from one side of the scene to the other, we'd need to use 12 of them!

One of the easiest ways programmers save time and effort is by using their version of a Repeat block. You line up a command or a list of commands and then choose how many times they should be repeated, meaning the whole list of commands will run and then run again. But for now, we'll just use Repeat to make it easier to move more spaces at a time.

Choose Create New Story on the home screen and pick four characters to include in your story. For our example we'll use the ghost, the pink fox, the bird, and the octopus. Pick whichever scene you want — our story won't really be about the background where they are. For our example, we'll use the underwater scene with the seashell house.

Drag all four characters into a straight line across, starting with the ghost in the lower left corner. The ghost should be one square away from the left edge and the bottom edge. Line its friends up next to it along the bottom like they're going to race each other.

Click Edit under the ghost and drag these commands just as you see them here:

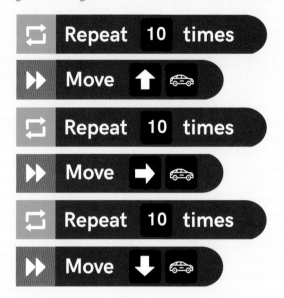

All our commands are lined up against the left side. But Repeat is a container, like a cup or a basket, so it needs to hold a command inside it. Touch and hold the first Move block and gently drag it up toward the Repeat block. You'll see that the Move block will scoot a little bit to the right, and the Repeat block will make a gray box around it. That's how you know the Move block is in the Repeat container.

So here's how your final list will look:

That's all for the ghost. Now, click on the pink fox at the top, and make these commands:

Be careful, because the Wait blocks aren't in the Repeats. You might find it easier to drag all the commands into place and then put the Move blocks into the Repeats one at a time. Whatever works best for you!

Next is the bird. These commands are really similar to what we just did for the pink fox:

And finally for the octopus:

Press the Play button and see what happens. Your characters should swim up and then stop in a diagonal line, then swim across and stop in a diagonal line, and finally swim down to the other side of the seashell house. Instead of doing 20 or more Move blocks for each character, we used 3 and told them to repeat.

In the example, we used Wait blocks to make sure all the characters caught up before we started the next leg of our race. Try taking the Wait blocks out of each character's command list — touch and hold the block, and then drag it toward the right side to remove it.

Now, don't change any of the Repeat or Move blocks, but click into the Move blocks and choose different speeds. Instead of them all being car speed, make some turtle speed and some rabbit speed. When you press Play, what happens? One character will pull ahead, then after a turn, the other characters will try to catch up.

REPEAT

Repeat just saved us a lot of work dragging Move blocks into our command list over and over. Why do the same small task by hand a million times, if you can tell the computer once and let it do the rest of the work? This makes everything faster.

If you've learned how to multiply or divide in school, you've already learned a kind of Repeat block. When you multiply 5 × 5, you're adding 5 + 5 + 5 + 5 + 5. Multiplying is less work to get the same answer. It doesn't make too big of a difference when you're using small numbers, but for adults who work in jobs like engineering or science or even as managers for stores, having a simpler way to do their math with big numbers is a huge time savings.

But Repeat blocks don't just save time. Remember when we told a story where we needed five Move blocks in a row? Each new Move block has new parameters that we have to get just right for our story to work. And each time you make more work for yourself, you have a new chance to accidentally make a mistake.

That's not just you — it's human nature! Everyone makes mistakes sometimes. When you do one small task 100 times, you're more likely to make a mistake than if you do one big task. So in our third story, when we used Repeat blocks to help our characters move, we changed their speed in just one block instead of 10.

If you go back into that story, you can even use one huge Repeat block to include all the different action, and repeat the whole story up to 10 times! All you have to do is add one block. Isn't that amazing?

BROADCAST

Do you know what a broadcast is? All television used to be sent through the air, like radio still is. If you've heard stories about the time in history when people had only three channels to watch, these were broadcast channels! Every TV had an antenna to receive a signal from the air. Radios still work this way, and even satellite radio gets a signal from the air.

For our block code, Broadcast is a way for one character to tell another character to do something. This idea is a little tricky, but we all use the same idea in our regular lives every day. In class, your teacher asks a question and then looks, with hope, toward the students. The question and the look together are a broadcast that tells you it's time to think about raising your hand!

Talking with your friends or family is the same thing. If someone is making dinner downstairs, and you're upstairs, they might call up the stairs to tell you dinner is ready. When you get that broadcast, you go downstairs to eat dinner. It's a signal for you to take action.

What are some other broadcasts that happen in our daily lives?

Some are more passive, which means you just watch or listen to them without taking action yourself. You might watch videos on YouTube where creators talk directly to the audience, but they usually don't tell you to do something, besides Like and Subscribe. That's still a broadcast.

But the video host might ask you to say something in a comment. Or you might follow someone on Instagram who does a poll where you can vote, but you just touch a button. It's not very complicated to do what they ask or suggest.

When you talk with friends or play sports or games, there are a lot of kinds of broadcasts. When someone has the basketball, they look around for someone to pass to, which is sending a signal with their eyes. If a friend seems upset and tells you a sad story about something bad that happens, you might get a signal that your friend wants to be comforted.

What do all these situations have in common? Well, everyone is watching or listening for something to happen that changes the situation for them. And that's how we use a Broadcast block in our code.

In our first three stories, we used lots of Wait For Time blocks to keep our stories going at the right speed. We also used them to let characters catch up when others were talking. Sometimes, we can use Broadcast to make this job easier.

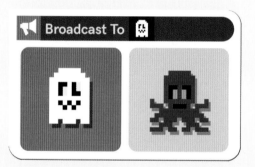

There are two parts of a whole Broadcast. First, the character sending the signal needs a Broadcast block. Let's say we have a ghost signaling to an octopus. In the ghost's command list, we might see:

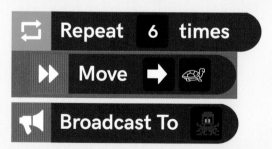

In the octopus's command list, we'll start by dragging in a Wait For Broadcast block.

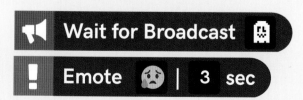

So the ghost will approach the octopus, and the octopus will make a face to show it's scared!

VISIBLE

Imagine a scary haunted house. A group of friends are investigating the house. Suddenly, the lights flash on and off, and a ghost appears in the room with them! Ghosts aren't real, but they help us understand our next command. A Visible block lets you choose whether or not we can see a character in the scene. The character is still there when it's not visible — you drag it into the scene like all the others. It has a list of commands that it follows. In fact, it will still do everything in the command list while it's invisible.

Remember our experiment with four characters who run a race together? If you made that story as you read the instructions, you can go back now and drop in a couple of Visible blocks to see it in action. In our example, we even used a ghost!

Drag and drop a Visible block toward the top of the command list for just one character. Here's the command list from our ghost in that story:

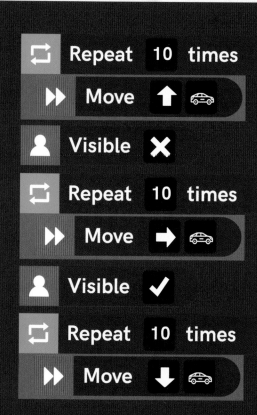

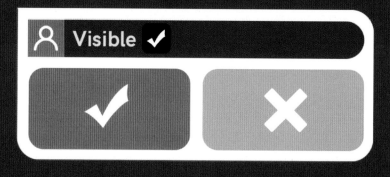

Play the story again and see what happens. The ghost will make the trip to the top of the screen, then disappear. After a few seconds, it will reappear on the other side of the screen, then travel down to the bottom to finish the race. All the Visible block does is change how the character looks on the screen. Everything else still happens!

Having the power to appear and disappear like a ghost gives us a really good tool for telling stories.

PLAY & EMOTE

Now let's talk about what these two blocks are and how we can use them.

Play

The Learn to Code app comes with a bunch of different sound effects. There's no set length of any of the sounds, so they're all a little different. When you use a Play block, the rest of your commands will keep going while the sound plays in the background. (You can use a Wait For Time to pause the action if you want.)

When we programmed our bear to look for its keys inside the dark cave:

...

 Play: Footstep 1

...

The Wait block helps to make sure the bear stays inside the cave while the sound effect finishes playing. If you wanted the bear to walk around, visible, with the footstep sounds, you'd need to use the right timing. How could you do this?

Try adding this code to a story:

 Play: Footstep 1

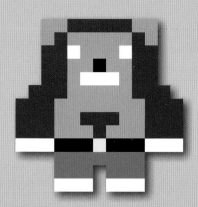

When you press Play, your character will stop moving before the footstep sounds are finished. But if you try this instead:

Play: Footstep 1

Now, when you press Play, the timing is a lot closer. Using sounds is really fun, and it can add a lot to your story. But you'll need to try different things and play your scene to see how they work. (If you know any grownups who work as coders, ask them about how much they have to "guess and check" their work. It's probably a lot.)

Just like with our color palette, we're limited to a certain number of sound effects to use. Sometimes, there might not be an ideal sound for what you want in your story. What can you do? Play through the sounds and imagine what that moment in your story will be like. Chances are good that you'll find a different sound that works for what you're imagining, and it might even be funnier, scarier, or otherwise better than what you originally wanted.

Emote

The word "emote" was made by just cutting off the end of "emotion." Sadness, happiness, confusion, and fear are all emotions. But even these big words include many more slightly different feelings. Sometimes, we feel sad while we're happy — like going to a birthday party when a friend has to stay home sick. Emotions get complicated.

In the app, you have your choice of four emotes: happy, sad, rolling eyes, and angry. In the story where the fox waits while the bear looks for its keys, we used eyeroll emote to show that the fox is fed up with waiting for his friend. But the fox isn't mad — you get the feeling the bear loses its keys a lot. Our friends do the same things over and over and we can almost predict it like we're psychic.

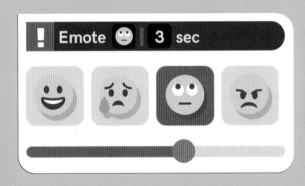

Like Play blocks, Emote blocks don't stop other commands from happening. Your character will still move around while it's emoting. So if you want an emote to pause the rest of the action, you need to use a Wait For Time block, too. You could even have a character show changing feelings. Our story with the bear and fox ended with the fox rolling its eyes, but what if we did these commands instead?

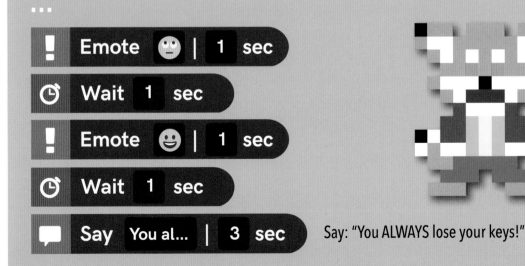

Say: "You ALWAYS lose your keys!"

Now, the fox rolls its eyes, then smiles, showing that it really does like its friend the bear.

CODING FOR REAL

Most people who work as professional coders have really specific tasks that they work on. They might help to fix bugs, or problems, in big pieces of software that companies need to use. The same way we worked on stories and checked if they were doing what we wanted, coders run programs and check to see what's happening.

Some coding languages are more like what we used in our app. A language called Scratch lets you do more complicated things with the same kind of drag-and-drop blocks. Some languages let you draw objects and then add code to them directly, or draw objects that you link with your code later.

Other coding languages are all made of words that you type by hand. These can be hard to use, because you need to spell everything right, use the right number of spaces or commas or quotation marks, and all kinds of other things. But professional coders have programs where they type code like this, and the computer helps them check their spelling and details.

A lot of young coders look for jobs where they can do the newest, coolest kind of programming. That's okay to do, but many coders work on older languages. Programming is like cars. Some people drive brand new cars, but more people drive older cars. Some coders can even make more money because they know old languages.

If drawing characters and making stories about them inspired you to want to make your own bigger stories or even games, there are cool programs that can help you do that. One called RPG Maker has been used to make games like *Rakuen* and *To the Moon*. If you play these games, you'll see how much they're just really good stories underneath all the other stuff.

Think about how you've used this one single app. The stories you want to tell, the characters you want to draw — those are unique to you, meaning every kid who uses the app does it a little bit differently.

Coders are the same way. Some make a living as coders, meaning it's their job and they get paid. Some have other jobs but work on games and projects in their free time. There's no one way you have to learn to code.

Written by Nicole Sulgit and Beth Taylor
Photo styling by Nick LaShure and Nicole Sulgit
Photography by Christopher Hiltz, Nick LaShure and Nicole Sulgit
Additional images from Shutterstock.com

Louis Weber, CEO
Publications International, Ltd.
8140 Lehigh Avenue
Morton Grove, IL 60053

First printing
Manufactured in China.
03/2021 Guangdong

8 7 6 5 4 3 2 1

SAFETY WARNING

All of the experiments and activities in this book MUST be performed with adult supervision. All projects contain a degree of risk, so carefully read all instructions before you begin and make sure that you have safety materials such as goggles, gloves, etc. Also make sure that you have safety equipment, such as a fire extinguisher and first aid kit, on hand. You are assuming the risk of any injury by conducting these activities and experiments. Publications International, Ltd. will not be liable for any injury or property damage.

Let's get social!

◉ @Publications_International

🅕 @PublicationsInternational

🅕 @BrainGames.TM

www.pilbooks.com

CONTENTS

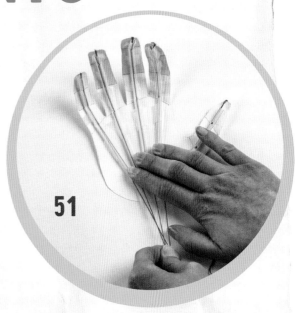

51

16

A plant, a person, a Pomeranian...

What do they have in common?

They are all alive! In this book, we look at the varied forms of life that exist on Earth and all around you. How do they work? How do they grow? What do they need to thrive?

Some forms of life, like miniscule bacteria, are simple.

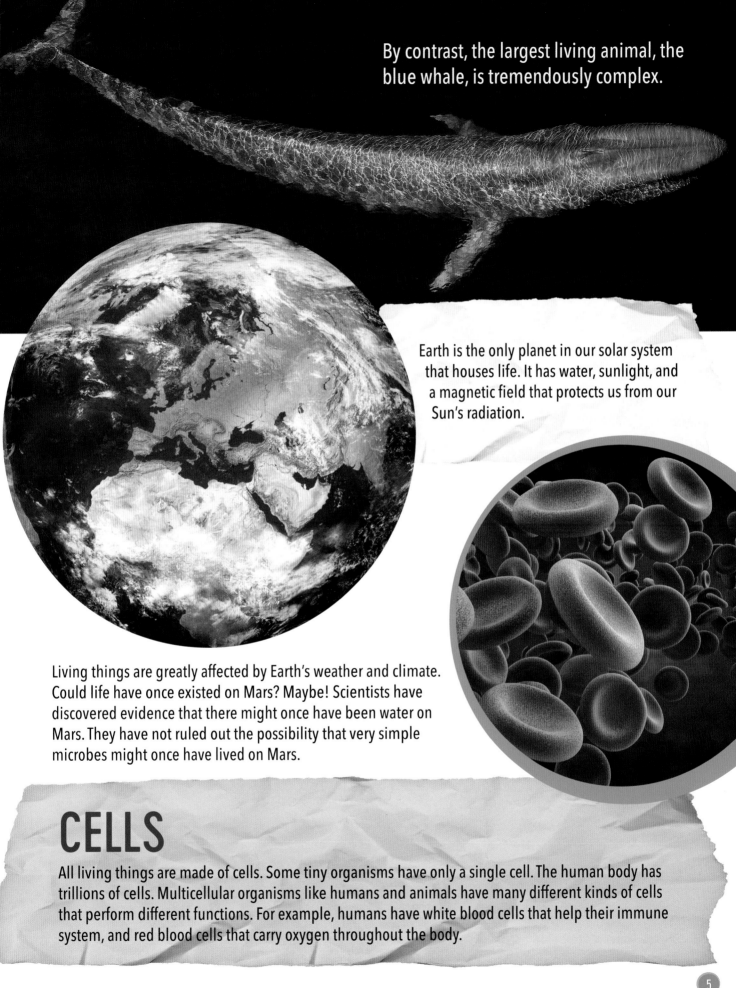

By contrast, the largest living animal, the blue whale, is tremendously complex.

Earth is the only planet in our solar system that houses life. It has water, sunlight, and a magnetic field that protects us from our Sun's radiation.

Living things are greatly affected by Earth's weather and climate. Could life have once existed on Mars? Maybe! Scientists have discovered evidence that there might once have been water on Mars. They have not ruled out the possibility that very simple microbes might once have lived on Mars.

CELLS

All living things are made of cells. Some tiny organisms have only a single cell. The human body has trillions of cells. Multicellular organisms like humans and animals have many different kinds of cells that perform different functions. For example, humans have white blood cells that help their immune system, and red blood cells that carry oxygen throughout the body.

MANY KINDS OF LIFE

The study of life on earth is called biology. Biology has many branches. Zoologists study animals, while microbiologists study tiny organisms. Geneticists study genes and how animals and other living things pass on traits to their children.

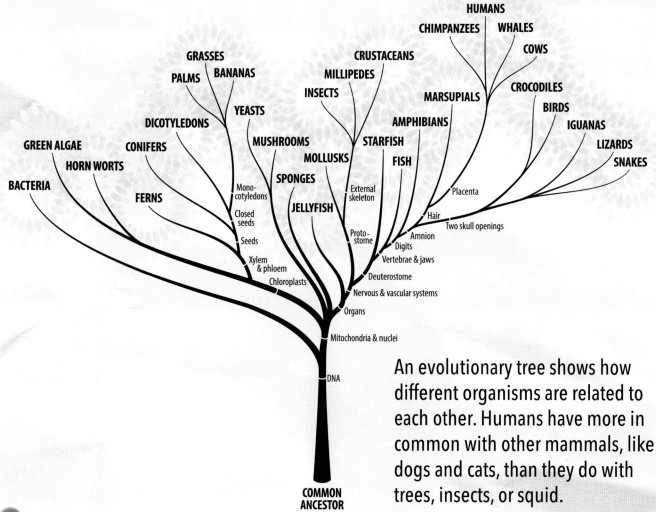

GRASSES
PALMS   BANANAS
DICOTYLEDONS
YEASTS
GREEN ALGAE   CONIFERS
HORN WORTS
MUSHROOMS
BACTERIA   FERNS
MOLLUSKS
SPONGES
JELLYFISH

Mono-cotyledons
Closed seeds
Seeds
Xylem & phloem
Chloroplasts

CRUSTACEANS
MILLIPEDES
INSECTS

STARFISH
FISH

AMPHIBIANS

External skeleton

Proto-stome
Digits
Vertebrae & jaws
Deuterostome
Nervous & vascular systems
Organs
Mitochondria & nuclei
DNA

HUMANS
CHIMPANZEES   WHALES
COWS
CROCODILES
MARSUPIALS
BIRDS
IGUANAS
LIZARDS
SNAKES

Placenta
Hair   Two skull openings
Amnion

COMMON ANCESTOR

An evolutionary tree shows how different organisms are related to each other. Humans have more in common with other mammals, like dogs and cats, than they do with trees, insects, or squid.

Animals can be vertebrates or invertebrates. Vertebrates like fish, lizards, birds, and humans have backbones. Invertebrates like insects, octopuses, and sponges do not.

CLASSIFICATION OF ANIMALS

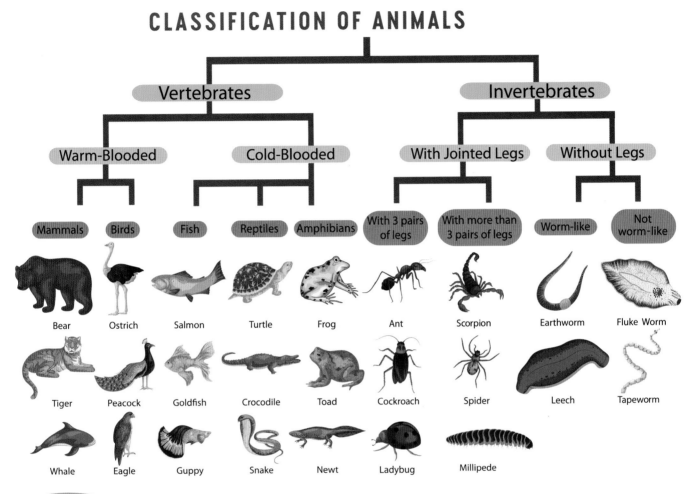

Insects are some of the most diverse animals on Earth. There are many different kinds of insects. And there may be as many as 10 quintillion individual insects alive right now!

The fossil record shows that plants existed on land at least 420 million years ago. Some scientists think they moved from water to land even earlier than that.

NATURE WALK

How many different kinds of living things can you see in a 20-minute walk?

MATERIALS

- Pen or pencil
- Notebook
- Colored pencils or crayons (optional)
- Camera (optional)

Spend 20 minutes outdoors—in your neighborhood, in a nearby park, or just in your backyard. Take notes in your notebook of all the kinds of life you see. If you don't know the name of a bug, bird, or plant, then describe it, draw it in your notebook, or snap a photograph. You can go as a family, and see who spots the most living things!

HOW MANY...

INSECTS? **TREES?**
FLOWERS? **BIRDS?**
BUSHES? **PEOPLE?**
WEEDS? **PETS?**

Do you hear any animals that you do not see? For example, you might hear a cicada humming, a frog croaking, or a bird chirping, even if you do not spot it.

SAFETY NOTES

1. If you are hiking in a place with ticks, wear a long-sleeved shirt and tuck your pants into your boots. Check your backpack and clothes when you get home.

2. Be careful of poison ivy and its relatives.

WHAT PLANTS NEED

Humans and other animals eat food, which gives them energy that they use to function. Plants make their own food through a process called photosynthesis.

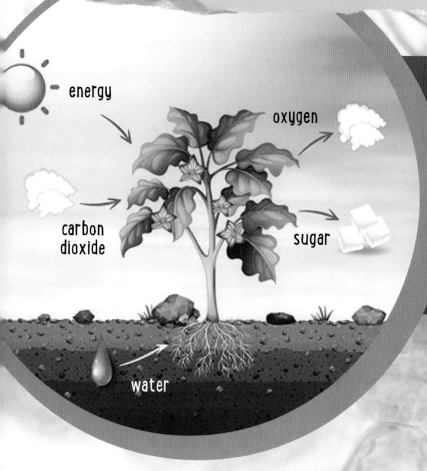

energy

oxygen

carbon dioxide

sugar

water

THREE NEEDS

Plants take in sunlight, water, and a gas called carbon dioxide. In the process of photosynthesis, they transform these into a sugar called glucose that they use for energy, as well as oxygen. Plants provide a lot of the oxygen in our air that humans need to breathe!

WHY PLANTS ARE GREEN

The green color in many plants is due to a pigment called chlorophyll. Without chlorophyll, plants could not absorb sunlight.

WHY DO LEAVES CHANGE COLORS?

In fall, trees stop making food. The level of chlorophyll in their leaves lessens. As it does, we can see the other pigments that were hidden by the chlorophyll. During the winter, the tree stores its nutrients in its roots.

Some simple plants like mosses are non-vascular, and do not have specialized tissues.

VASCULAR PLANTS

Most plants, including all flowering plants, have specific types of tissues that help them move water and nutrients throughout the plant. A tissue called phloem transports sugars, while xylem transports water.

LOVING THE SUN

When a living thing seeks out light, scientists call it "phototropic." In some plants, like tulips, phototropism is very noticeable. On pages 14–15, we'll set up an experiment that shows phototropism in action.

BEAN IN A BAG

How long does it take for a bean to grow? What does it need to grow into a plant?

MATERIALS

- Dried beans*
- Paper towel
- Plastic baggie

*We used pinto beans, but you can use any dried bean you have available, including black beans, lentil beans, navy beans, or mung beans.

Step 1

Fold a paper towel into quarters. Wet the paper towel, then squeeze out extra water. Place it in a plastic baggie.

Step 2

Place a bean or beans into the bag, on top of the towel. Leave the plastic bag unsealed so air can get into it. Place the bag somewhere where the beans can get light.

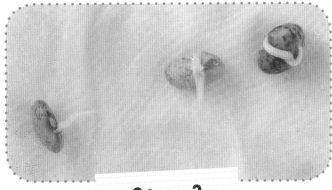

Step 3

After a few days, your beans will begin to sprout! In this photograph, the beans have been in the bag for four days.

Step 4

Once the beans begin to sprout, they grow quickly. These beans have been in the bag for one week.

Step 5

You can transfer your beans to a small container of soil. This container has about 8 bean sprouts. Soil will help your bean sprouts grow even faster.

QUICK GROWTH

When you think of a seed, you might think of sunflower seeds or pumpkin seeds. But the beans you eat on a burrito are seeds too! Seeds contain all the nutrients a plant needs for growth. Once you add water and light, you're on your way. Here are some further experiments to try:

- What kind of bean sprouts fastest? Grow a few bean varieties, making sure they're grown in the same conditions in terms of water, light, space, and air.

- How does light affect growth? Put one bean in a sunny window, another in a shady area, and another in a closet and see how light conditions affect growth.

SHOEBOX PLANT

Do you like mazes? Create a maze for your bean sprout plant and see how well it grows.

MATERIALS

- Bean sprout(s) in small pot with soil
- Empty shoebox
- Two sturdy card pieces
- Scissors
- Ruler
- Tape

Step 1

Plant a young bean sprout in a small container with soil. Decorate your shoebox if you'd like.

Step 2

Cut a hole in the top of the shoebox.

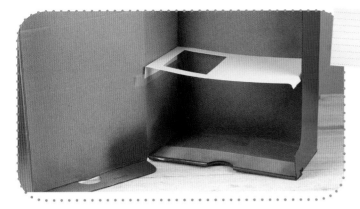

Step 3

Measure the width of the shoebox with your ruler. Cut a piece of sturdy card into a rectangular shape so that it is slightly wider than the shoebox. Cut a window on one side of the card. Fold the edges of the card to make flaps, place the card inside the shoebox, and tape the flaps to the box.

Step 4

Cut another piece of card and place it in the box. The window in the card should be on the opposite side.

Step 5

Place your plant inside the box. Close the lid on the box and place it in a location with light.

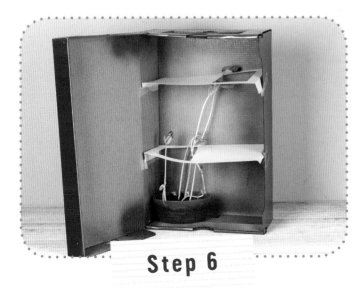

Step 6

Check your box every few days.
Water the plant if the soil is dry.

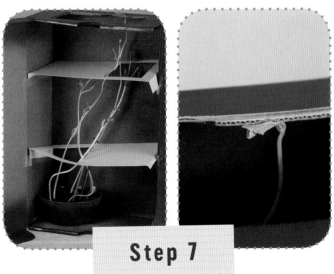

Step 7

How long does it take for your plant to reach the top of the box?

TREE
TRANSPIRATION

A tree's roots gather water, which moves up the plant to its leaves. Small pores on the leaf release water to the air.

MATERIALS

- Large clear bag
- Tape
- Scissors
- Rock
- Tree

Step 1

Drop the rock in the bag, then place the bag over as many leaves as possible.

Step 2

Tape the bag to hold it in place.

Step 3

The rock weighs down the bag, allowing the water that collects to drip down.

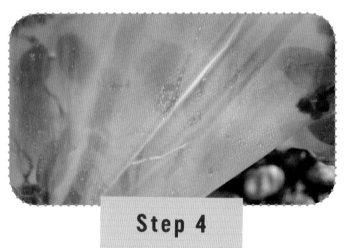

Step 4

Leave the bag for 24 hours. If you check occasionally, you will see water droplets begin to bead on the bag's surface.

Step 5

Cut a corner off and collect water. Don't drink the water and make sure to remove the bag from the tree!

COLORFUL FLOWERS

Can a white flower become green or red or blue? It can, with a little food coloring, water, and time.

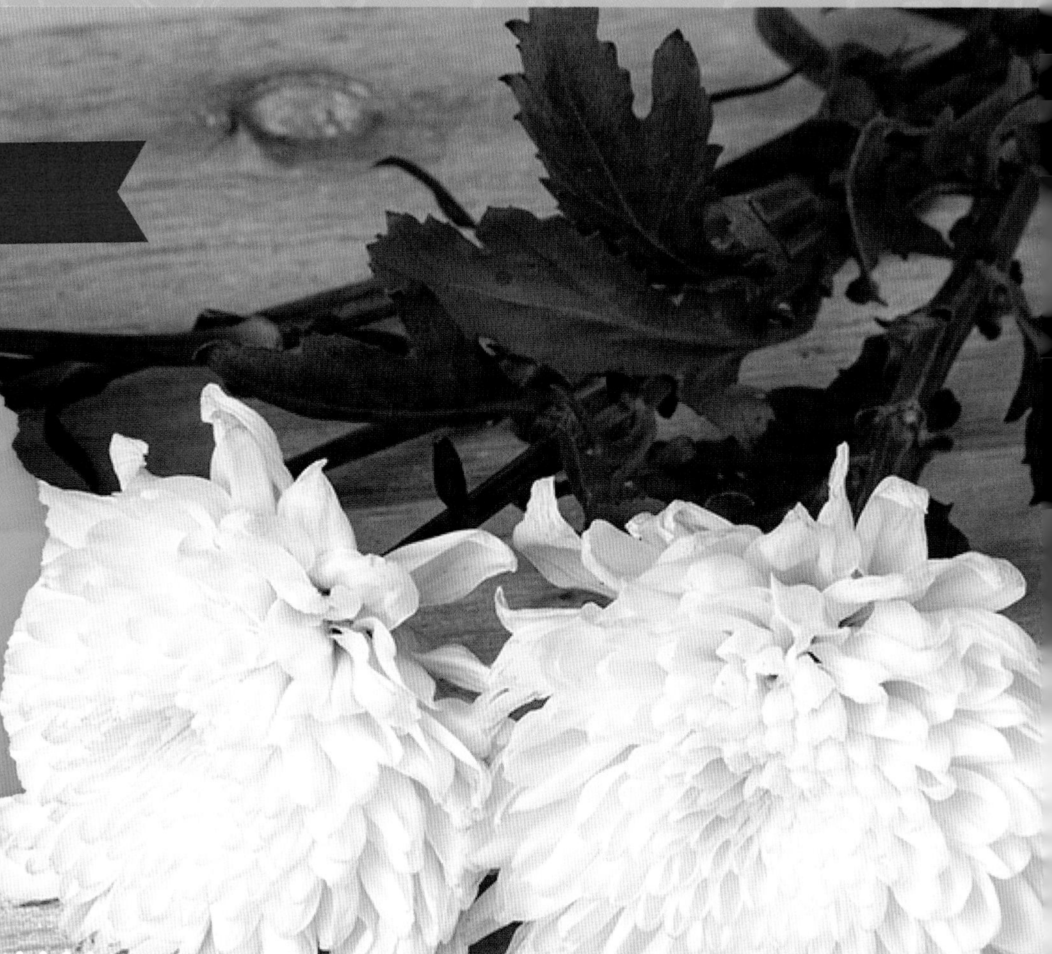

MATERIALS

- White flowers
- Food coloring
- Glasses or vases
- Water
- Scissors
- Tape

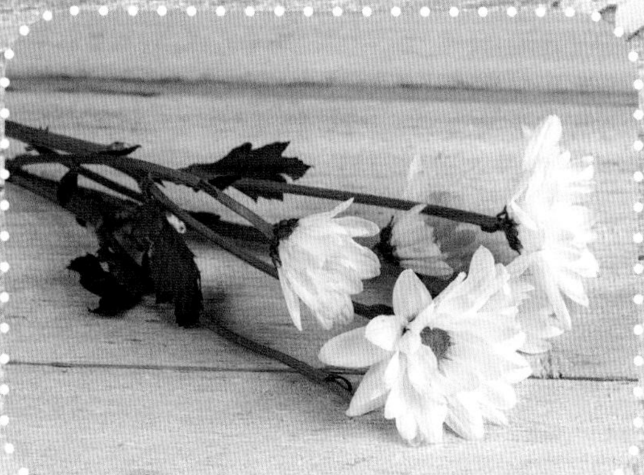

Step 1

Decide what kind of flower to use. We ran our experiments with carnations, chrysanthemums, and daisies.

Step 2

Cut the stem to the size of your vase or glass. Strip away any excess leaves.

Step 3

Add a few drops of food coloring to the water.

Step 4

Add your flower to the water and set it someplace where it will get light.

Step 5

Try different flowers in different colors! For extra fun, carefully cut a stem into two and place each half of the stem into a glass with a different color. *What do you think will happen to that flower? Do you think the colors will combine, resulting in a purple flower? Or do you think you'll end up with a flower that is half red and half blue?*

Step 6

If the flower has a hard time staying upright, use tape to secure it.

It will take several hours at a minimum to begin changing colors. For best results leave the flower in the glass for several days.

The flower with the split stem will begin to show two different colors. The half with the stem in blue water will turn blue, while the half with the stem in red water will turn red.

HOW DOES IT WORK?

A plant's stem carries water and nutrients to the rest of the plant. The colorful water slowly travels up the stem to change the color of the flower's petals through a process called capillary action. If you tried a variety of flowers, which flower changed colors fastest? Which colors worked best?

Florists dye flowers with several different methods, including the absorption method. They also use floral spray paint. Blue roses, for example, do not occur in nature. While some blue-ish rose variations have been created via genetic engineering, many blue roses are simply white roses that have been dyed blue.

You may see flowers with metallic tinges or glitter added to them for holidays such as New Year's Day or St. Patrick's Day. You may be able to find spray paint that can be used safely on flowers at a local craft store.

SPORES, SEEDS, AND CONES

You grew a bean plant from a seed. How do plants reproduce in nature?

SPORES

Some more primitive plants, like ferns and mosses, produce through spores. Spores develop on the plant. Under certain conditions—like warm, dry air—the spores are expelled from the plant and drift on the wind until they land elsewhere. If the spores land in a moist, shady place, the spore may go through a process where a new plant can grow. Because the conditions need to be just right for growth, a lot of spores don't become new plants.

CONES

Conifers reproduce using their cones. Each plant has two kinds of cones, male and female. The male cone produces pollen, which the wind carries away. If some of the pollen reaches a female cone, it creates a seed. Eventually, the seed is carried away by the wind to land where it may grow into a new plant.

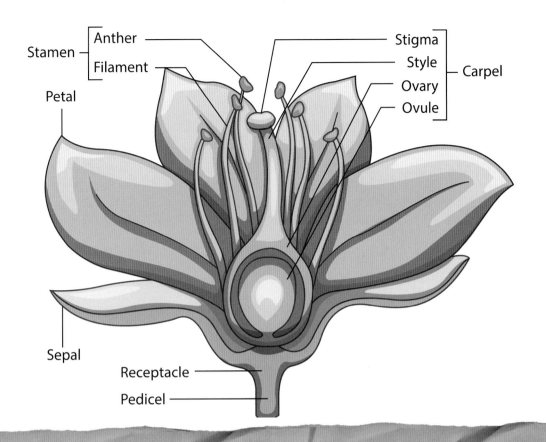

Stamen
Anther
Filament
Petal
Stigma
Style
Ovary
Ovule
Carpel
Sepal
Receptacle
Pedicel

FLOWERING PLANTS AND SEEDS

Flowering plants reproduce through seeds. Flowering plants have parts that both make and receive pollen. An animal such as a hummingbird or an insect such as a bee picks up a grain of pollen from a plant's anther. If it carries it to the stigma of that plant or another plant of the same type, the plant may go through a process that leads to a new seed growing.

A bean plant is an angiosperm—a flowering plant.

MAKE YOUR OWN SEEDS

In autumn, maple trees release a "samara" that carries the seed far from the tree. You might know it as a "helicopter" or "whirligig." You can throw them up in the air and watch them spin to the ground! Make your own samara with construction paper.

MATERIALS

- Construction or tissue paper
- Scissors
- Glue
- Seeds such as sunflower seeds or raisins
- String (optional)

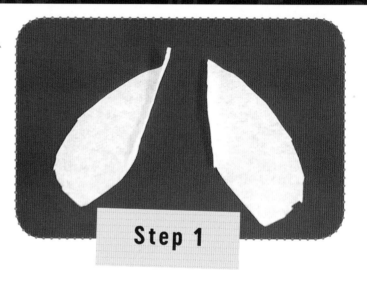

Step 1

Cut out two identical wing shapes for your samara from construction paper or tissue paper.

Step 3

Throw your samara in the air and see if it spins to the ground! You can also create a samara with two wings and join it with string.

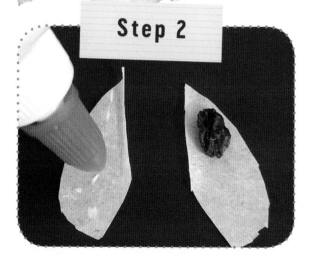

Step 2

Place a seed at one end of one wing shape. With small dabs of glue, glue the two wing shapes together with the seed at one end.

NATURE AND TECHNOLOGY

Do you have a shoe with velcro straps? Velcro was created by a Swiss engineer named George de Mestral in the 1940s. He was inspired by burrs that attached to his clothing and his dog's fur when he went hiking.

Burrs protect a plant. Because they attach to objects and are carried along, they are also a form of seed dispersal.

Have you ever bought seedless grapes? One way to grow a plant is to take a cutting, a piece from an existing plant such as its root, and put it somewhere where it can grow. The new plant is basically a clone of the existing plant.

HOW ANIMALS MOVE

There are dozens of words for how animals move. Some soar, while others wriggle. Some crawl, while others hop and leap. Some fly, while a few glide. Some animals scarcely move at all!

Flying squirrels don't really fly. But they can glide, taking off from one tree to another. Their patagium—the membrane that looks like a wing—acts like a parachute and helps keep them in the air.

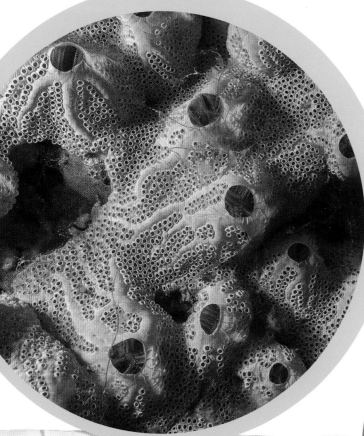

Sponges stay rooted in a single spot all their lives.

Jellyfish contract and relax the muscles in the top part of their body, the bell, to move. This forces out water in a jet behind them, which propels them forward.

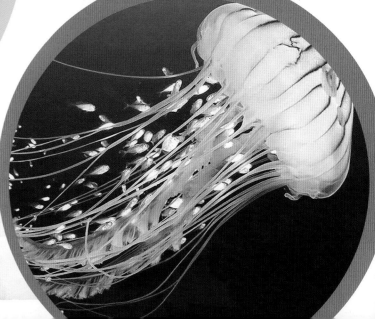

Elephants may live most of their lives walking on land, but they can swim too!

Frogs can jump away from danger. Their bones, muscles, and joints have evolved to help them leap.

Humans are bipedal. We walk on two feet! Can you name other animals that are bipedal?

HOW FISH SWIM

Fish swim with their whole bodies. They move their bodies in a wave, bending back and forth, which propels them through the water. Their tail fin, or caudal fin, helps them move.

WHAT DO FINS DO?

Many fish use their fins to steer. Some fish use their pectoral fins—the first set of fins—to move. Other fish use them more as brakes, or to help maneuver quickly in tight spaces.

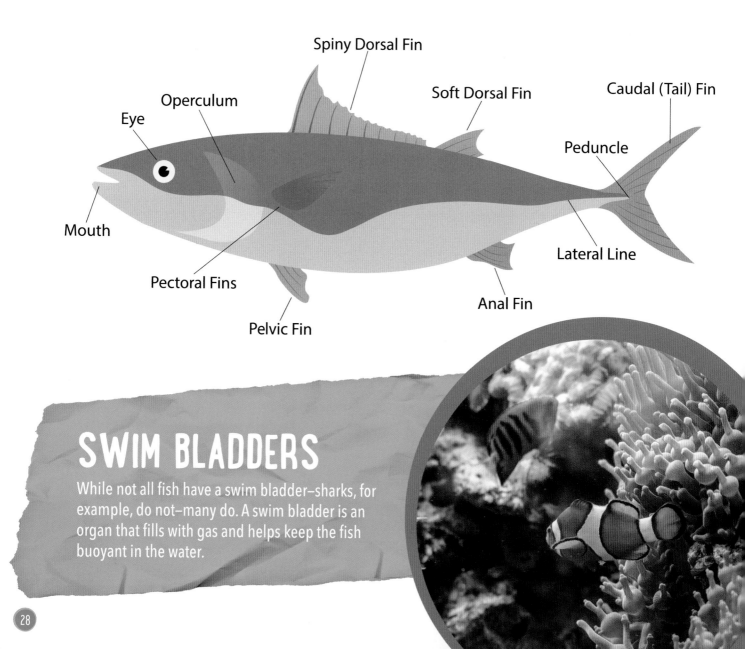

Spiny Dorsal Fin

Soft Dorsal Fin

Caudal (Tail) Fin

Operculum

Eye

Peduncle

Mouth

Pectoral Fins

Pelvic Fin

Anal Fin

Lateral Line

SWIM BLADDERS

While not all fish have a swim bladder—sharks, for example, do not—many do. A swim bladder is an organ that fills with gas and helps keep the fish buoyant in the water.

SWIM BLADDER

MATERIALS

- Sink
- Plastic bag that seals shut
- Penny

Step 1

Fill the sink with a few inches of water. Put a penny in the bag and seal it shut, without any air. Push it to the bottom of the sink. Then let go. The penny weighs down the bag and keeps it at least partially submerged in water.

Step 2

Take your bag out of the water. Open up one end, just a little, and blow into the bag to fill it with air. Seal it again.

Swim floaties that keep young kids buoyant in the water are acting like a fish's swim bladder.

Step 3

Submerge it in water. Push it down to the bottom of the sink, then let go. It immediately pops to the surface.

HOW BIRDS FLY

The bodies of birds have evolved to help them get, and stay, in the air. They have light bones with a honeycomb structure, strong chest muscles, and a streamlined body.

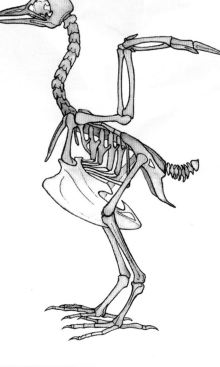

WINGS

Birds' wings are shaped so that more air flows above the wing than below the wing. This helps create a force called lift that counters the force of gravity.

FEATHERS

What do a rhino's horn and a bird's feathers have in common? They are both made of a substance called keratin–you have some in your nails, too! Keratin is a tough, fibrous protein.

TAKING IT EASY

When a bird glides along without flapping its wings, it is using less energy.

BIRD-WATCHING

How many birds can you see in an hour?

- Pen or pencil
- Notebook
- Binoculars (optional)
- Camera (optional)

Step 1

With the help of an adult, do a little bit of internet research on birds in your area. What birds can you expect to see at this time of year? What do they look like? Are any birds migrating through your area?

Step 2

Go to your backyard or a nearby park. If you live close to an arboretum or botanic garden, take a family trip.

Step 3

Sit relatively still for an hour or so, noting in your notebook which birds you see in the sky and whether you see any birds in trees near you.

HOW MANY BIRDS DO YOU SEE? CAN YOU IDENTIFY THEM?

DO YOU SEE A BIRD TAKE OFF INTO FLIGHT? HOW DO THEY MOVE THEIR WINGS AS THEY DO SO?

DO YOU SEE A BIRD SOARING ON AN AIR CURRENT?

DO SOME BIRDS SEEM TO FLAP THEIR WINGS MORE? DOES IT HAVE ANYTHING TO DO WITH SIZE?

HOW SNAKES SLITHER

Snakes can not only move without arms and legs, they can move quickly! Snakes can strike in milliseconds. So how do they do it? Snakes actually have several different ways of moving.

SERPENTINE

Most snakes rely on a method of locomotion where they move their body back and forth in an s-shape, like a wave. It's also called undulation. They start off by pushing themselves against a rock or branch, or even just a bump in the ground.

SIDEWINDING

Some snakes have the ability to move in a sidewinding motion. They use this in slick areas such as mud where serpentine motion would be difficult. They use their muscles to throw their heads forward. Their bodies follow in a sideways manner.

CONCERTINA

In narrow spaces like tunnels, snakes can inch forward using this accordion-like motion, where they move the front part of their body forward, and then pull the back of their bodies behind. They can climb this way, too.

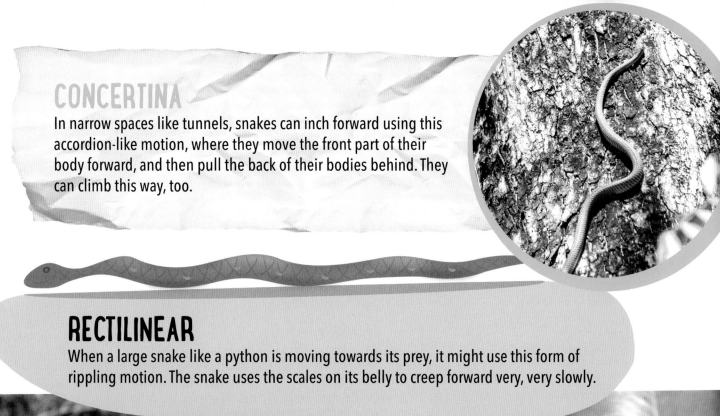

RECTILINEAR

When a large snake like a python is moving towards its prey, it might use this form of rippling motion. The snake uses the scales on its belly to creep forward very, very slowly.

Black mamba snakes are very fast. They can move at speeds of 10 miles per hour.

The Sri Lankan flying snake is one of several snakes that can "fly." They can't really fly, but they can glide from tree to tree.

Snake scales are made of keratin, just like bird feathers and your fingernails.

HOW CHEETAHS RUN

The fastest land mammals, cheetahs sprint around 60 miles per hour—and top that speed for short distances. How do they do it?

A cheetah's skull is small in comparison to the other big cats. This means it weighs less and is more streamlined.

A cheetah's spine is flexible, helping it stretch out.

A cheetah's heart and lungs are large, enabling it to breathe efficiently.

A cheetah's semi-retractable claws give it good traction, just like running shoes with tread help humans run faster than dress shoes.

A cheetah's tail helps it steer so it can turn and maneuver quickly.

GREYHOUND VS. SIBERIAN HUSKY

Which animal is faster?

OSTRICH VS. RHINO

Answers:

1. Light, agile greyhounds are built for speed, and can run close to 45 miles per hour. A Siberian husky can't run as fast, with a top speed near 30 miles per hour, but they can run for hours at a speed of 10 miles per hour.

2. The ostrich (the fastest-running bird) wins with a top speed of over 40 miles per hour, but rhinos can move pretty fast, with a speed of about 32 miles per hour.

HOW ANIMALS STAY WARM

One way scientists classify animals is to say whether they are endothermic or ectothermic. In common terms, are they warm-blooded or cold-blooded?

Endotherms, or warm-blooded animals, are able to maintain a stable body temperature regardless of their environment. Mammals, including humans, are warm-blooded.

Some endotherms hibernate. Their metabolism slows down, and their body temperature drops. Arctic ground squirrels can have a body temperature close to freezing!

Ectotherms, or cold-blooded animals, are greatly affected by the temperature of the environment around them. Reptiles and amphibians are ectotherms. A reptile in the sun will have a higher body temperature than a reptile in the shade.

TAKE YOUR TEMPERATURE

Normal human temperatures are clustered around 98.6 degrees Fahrenheit, but they can fluctuate during the course of the day, and from person to person. What is your normal body temperature range?

MATERIALS

- Thermometer
- Paper
- Pencil

WHAT HAPPENS IF YOU TAKE IT AFTER DRINKING A HOT DRINK, OR A COOL ONE?

Step 1

Decide on three times that you will take your temperature every day for a week: one morning time, one afternoon time, and one evening time. You should not eat, drink, or exercise for a half hour before taking your temperature.

Step 2

On the first three days, take your temperature at the same three times and record the results. Is your temperature always the same? If not, when is it highest or lowest?

TAKE YOUR TEMPERATURE IMMEDIATELY AFTER EXERCISING FOR 20 MINUTES. DO YOU SEE A DIFFERENCE FROM A DAY YOU HADNT EXERCISED? WAIT A HALF HOUR AND TRY AGAIN.

Step 3

Once you have established a baseline, try experimenting with the afternoon or evening recording. What happens if you take your temperature right after eating a snack?

BLUBBER GLOVE

How do animals like whales, seals, and polar bears stay warm in cold water? Let's do an experiment to see.

- 4 disposable vinyl gloves
- Ice
- Lard, butter, or shortening
- Large mixing bowl
- Stopwatch or phone with a stopwatch function

Step 1

Fill a bowl with ice.

Step 2

Put on a glove, and submerge your hand in the ice. Have a friend, sibling, or parent start the stopwatch when you put your hand in.

Step 3

Remove your hand when the cold becomes uncomfortable. How long did you last?

Step 4

Put on a fresh pair of gloves and find a source of kitchen fat. We used lard here.

Step 5

Spread the fat over one of your hands, coating the glove.

Step 6

Place a clean glove over that hand. You now have a layer of fat between the two gloves.

Step 7

Back your hand goes in the ice!

Step 8

How long can you last this time? We doubled our time, from 45 seconds to close to two minutes. The layer of fat keeps your hand warm.

WHAT DOES BLUBBER DO?

Mammals that live in cold water have a thick layer of fat called blubber underneath their skin that keeps them warm. Blubber can be several inches thick—even up to a foot thick! In the experiment, the lard, a source of fat, acted like blubber to keep your hand warm. But blubber helps in other ways, too. It stores energy and helps animals float. Pretty cool for a layer of fat!

Blubber isn't the only adaptation that polar bears have. Their short, thick claws help provide traction on the ice. A polar bear's fur is very thick, too. Its fur and blubber trap heat so well that bears are hard to spot with infrared cameras.

Emperor penguins have not only blubber, but lots of feathers–more per square inch than any other bird.

Beluga whales live in Arctic and sub-Arctic regions. Unlike many whales, they don't have dorsal fins on their backs, which helps them keep a streamlined profile under the ice. Their white skin helps them camouflage themselves.

Ringed seals have thick claws that help them maintain holes in the ice to let them breathe.

CAMOUFLAGE

Animals can adapt to their surroundings in amazing ways. Camouflage can help a predator animal hunt, or a prey animal disguise itself and hide.

A leopard's spots help it blend into grasses. The alternating patterns of light and dark help it break up its outline and blend into shadows.

A number of insects look like twigs or plant parts, which will be overlooked by predators.

Some animals can change colors to blend into their surroundings very quickly. Octopuses have thousands of cells called chromatophores that help them change colors within seconds.

Do these two snakes look the same to you?

The one on the left, a scarlet kingsnake, is not venomous. Because it mimics the appearance of the dangerous, venomous coral snake on the right, other animals may leave it alone.

SPOT THE ANIMAL

Can you spot the animals in these pictures?

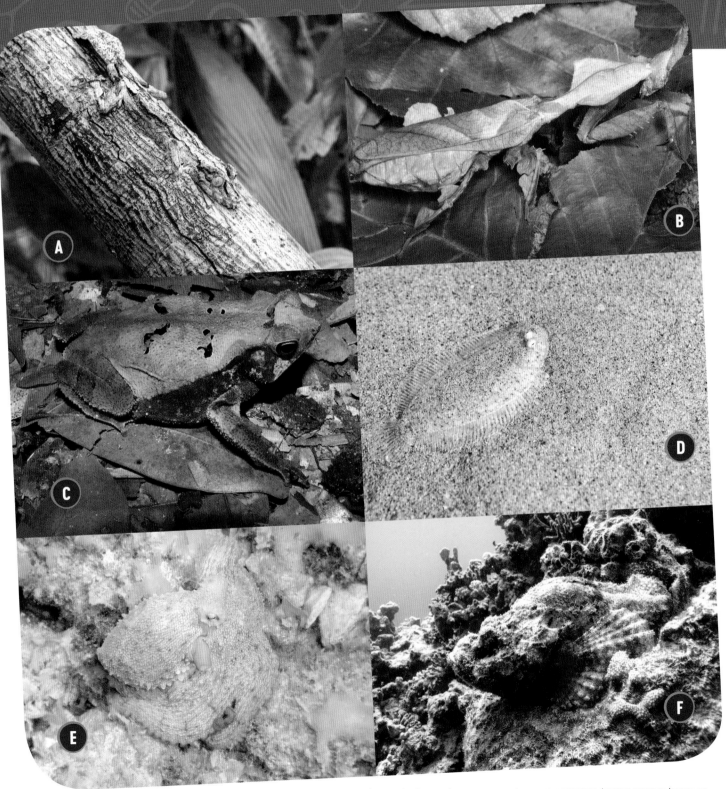

A. Gecko; B. Ghost mantis; C. Amazon leaf toad; D. Flat sole fish; E. Octopus; F. Scorpionfish

43

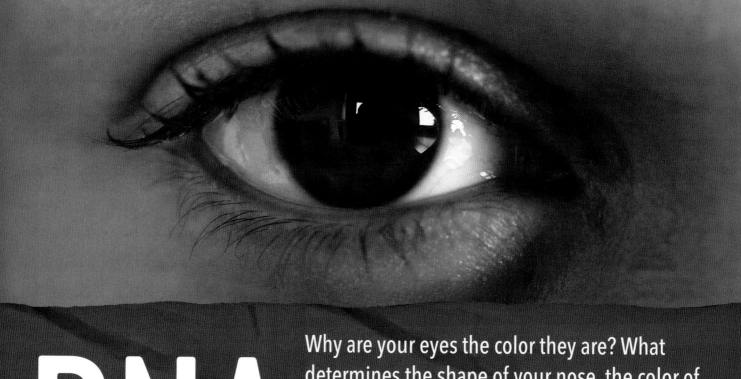

DNA

Why are your eyes the color they are? What determines the shape of your nose, the color of your hair, or whether you have an allergy? All these things are determined by your DNA. The cells in your body know how to function because they are getting instructions from your DNA.

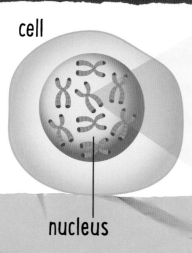

cell

nucleus

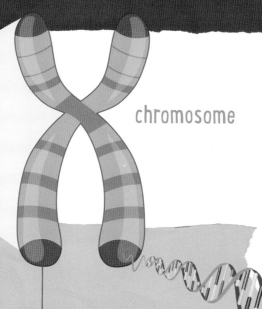

chromosome

telomere

DNA

DNA BASICS

- DNA stands for deoxyribonucleic acid.
- Every single cell of your body contains DNA.
- Humans aren't the only ones who have DNA. Every living thing has DNA.
- DNA is found within parts of your cells called chromosomes.
- Sections of DNA are called genes.

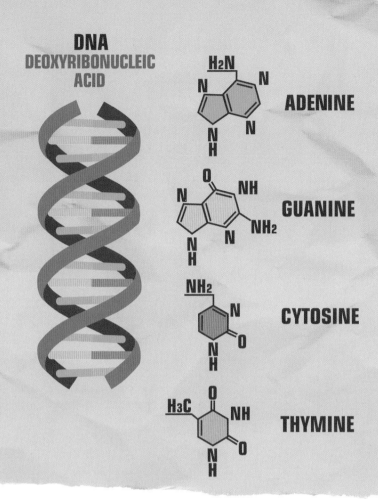

DNA
DEOXYRIBONUCLEIC ACID

ADENINE

GUANINE

CYTOSINE

THYMINE

THE FOUR BASES

DNA is built from four nucleotides, or bases: adenine, thymine, guanine, and cytosine. DNA forms in a very specific structure called a double helix, which has been compared to a ladder twisted into a spiral. The rungs of the ladder are two bases paired together. Adenine and thymine always pair together. Likewise, guanine is always paired with cytosine. The order of the bases act like a code, telling cells what proteins they should make.

MUTATIONS

Sometimes, somewhere in a chain of DNA, there is a change or mistake. Maybe a base is left out, or an extra base is put in. Mutations can cause diseases, but they can sometimes be beneficial.

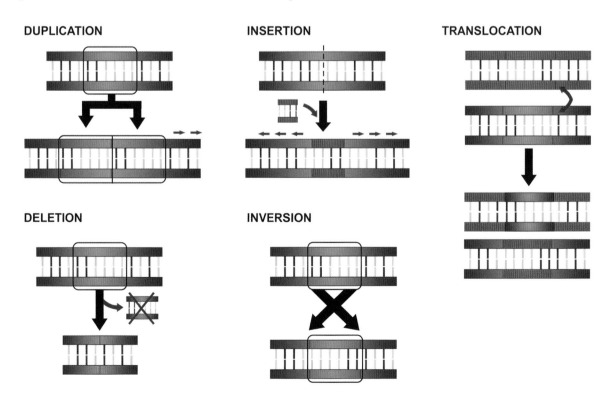

DUPLICATION

INSERTION

TRANSLOCATION

DELETION

INVERSION

DNA MODEL

Make a DNA model that looks like a twisted rope ladder, just like real DNA.

MATERIALS

- 4 different colored highlighters
- Colored tape (such as painter's tape)
- White paper
- Scratch paper
- Ruler
- Pencil with eraser
- Scissors

Step 1

Using a ruler and pencil, mark the white paper into about 25–30 strips, each ½ inch (1¼ cm) wide and 1¼ inches (3 cm) long.

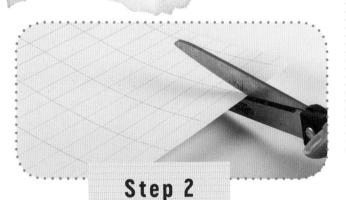

Step 2

Cut out the strips with scissors. These strips are the rungs of the ladder. Each one represents a pair of chemicals known as bases. There are only four different bases in DNA. You will use a different color highlighter to represent each of the bases.

Step 3

Erase any stray pencil marks on the strips. Fold each strip in half so that it consists of two equal-sized rectangles. The crease marks the dividing line between two bases. In real DNA, the two bases in each rung are held together by a chemical bond.

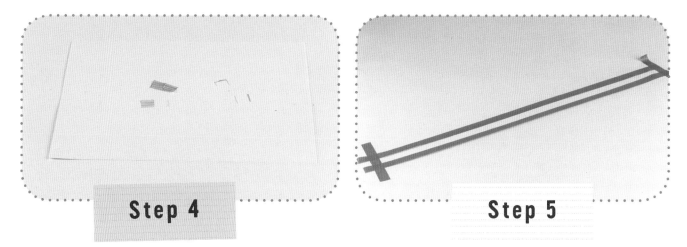

Step 4

Lay down scratch paper. Use 4 highlighter colors to represent the four bases in DNA. Color the paper strips so that one half is one color, the other half another. The colors should always be in pairs. For example, orange always goes with pink in our model. Color the strips identically front and back.

Step 5

Cut two strips of colored tape, each about 28 inches (70 cm) long, for the sides of the ladder. Lay them parallel to each other, sticky side up, with about ¾ inch (2 cm) between them. Use short pieces of tape to keep the two sides in place while you add the paper rungs.

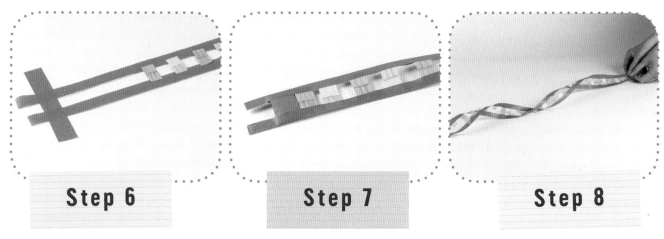

Step 6

Press paper rungs (base pairs), in any order, onto the two lengths of tape, leaving a gap of about a ½ inch (1 cm) between the rungs of the ladder.

Step 7

When you've used all the rungs, carefully fold both lengths of sticky tape lengthwise. This will hold the rungs between the folded pieces of tape.

Step 8

Gently twist the ladder into a spiral shape that's just like DNA itself. You can tape one end down or have another person hold it and twist from the other end. *Can you see why DNA is described as a double helix?*

HOW DOES IT WORK?

DNA (deoxyribonucleic acid) is found in the cells of all living things. DNA holds coded instructions that control how people, animals, and plants look and function. The bases—as represented in your model—are a code of instructions for how to make proteins. Proteins are needed for the structure, function, and regulation of a person's tissues and organs. A section of DNA that carries a recipe for a particular protein is called a gene. Humans have about 20,000–25,000 genes.

BREATHING

All animals need oxygen. But different animals take in oxygen in different ways.

Fish breathe in water, then expel it through their gills. As water travels out through the gills, it leaves oxygen that sustains the body.

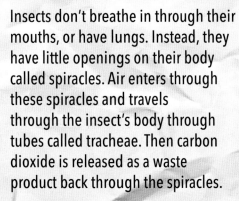

Mammals, including humans, have lungs. When humans go underwater, we hold our breath, storing oxygen in our lungs while we dive or swim. But some seals actually exhale before they dive. They store oxygen in their blood and muscles.

Insects don't breathe in through their mouths, or have lungs. Instead, they have little openings on their body called spiracles. Air enters through these spiracles and travels through the insect's body through tubes called tracheae. Then carbon dioxide is released as a waste product back through the spiracles.

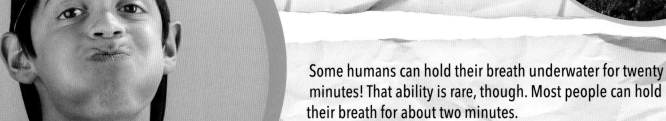

Some humans can hold their breath underwater for twenty minutes! That ability is rare, though. Most people can hold their breath for about two minutes.

YOUR LUNGS

MATERIALS

- Stopwatch
- Timer
- Pen and paper to take notes

Step 1

How many times do you inhale and exhale in a minute at rest? Set a timer for one minute and see how many times you inhale and exhale. Record that number.

Step 2

How does exercise affect your respiratory rate? Exercise for 20 minutes or so and then check how many times you inhale and exhale in a minute. It should be higher. Your body is working harder during exercise and needs more oxygen.

Step 3

Does age affect your respiratory rate? Check the respiratory rate (at rest) of the members of your household. See if they vary in any way.

Step 4

How long can you hold your breath? Take a big breath, start your stopwatch, and see!

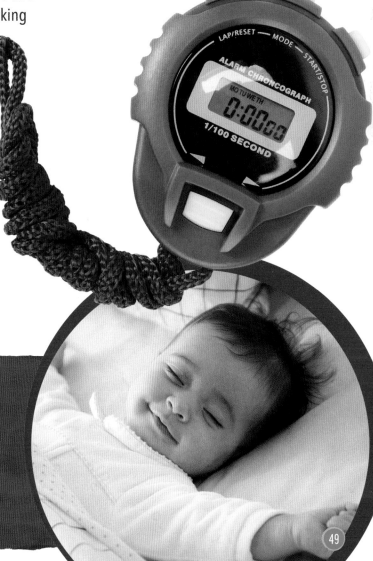

Most adults breathe about 12 to 20 times a minute, faster during exercise. Most kids have a higher respiratory rate—a 10-year-old may breathe up to 30 times a minute, a toddler may breathe up to 40 times a minute, and a baby may breathe up to 60 times a minute!

49

HOW HANDS WORK

Human hands are amazingly versatile and useful. With them, we discover textures, detect heat and cold, pick up and put down objects, wave away insects, hold pencils and phones, and more. Our opposable thumbs are especially useful in helping us grasp objects.

Opposable thumbs are not very common in the animal world, but humans aren't the only animals to have them. A number of primates have them. So do pandas–they use a sixth toe to grasp bamboo.

Fingertips have a lot of nerves and touch receptors. They can distinguish sensations that other patches of skin cannot. To demonstrate this, close your eyes. Have a friend or parent do the following, but scrambling the order:

- Touch the end of a pencil or chopstick lightly to your back. Ask how many pencil(s) are touching you.
- Touch two pencils or chopsticks side by side to your back. Ask how many pencil(s) are touching you.
- Touch two pencils or chopsticks to your back, about an inch apart, then two inches apart, then three. Ask how many pencil(s) are touching you each time.

Do the same tests with your fingertip and your wrist. How far apart did objects need to be before they registered as separate objects?

ARTIFICIAL HAND

Build an artificial hand out of drinking straws and string to mimic the way a real hand works.

MATERIALS

- Pen or marker
- 5 plastic straws
- Cardstock
- Tape
- String or embroidery floss
- Scissors
- Pencil

Step 1

Using a pencil, trace your hand onto a sheet of cardstock paper.

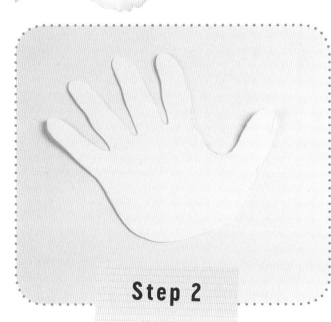

Step 2

Cut out your hand with scissors.

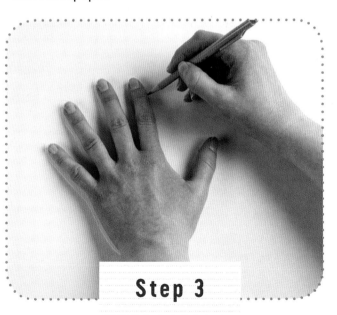

Step 3

Place your hand on the cutout and make pencil marks on either side of each joint. Joints are the places where fingers bend.

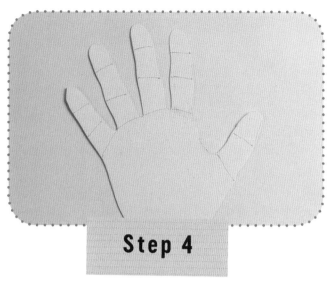

Step 4

Connect the pencil marks with lines where joints are located.

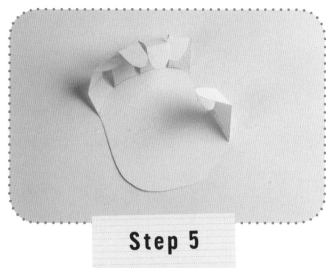

Step 5

Fold the fingers forward at each line.

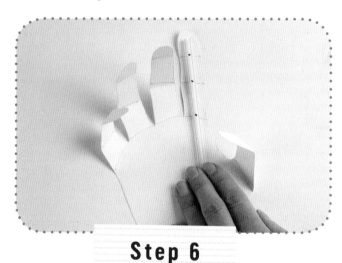

Step 6

Place a straw on top of a finger so that the top of the straw is a little below the top of the finger. With a marker or pen, mark the straw at each joint. Repeat for all other fingers.

the notches act as joints

Step 7

Use scissors to cut a triangular notch from the front of the straw where you marked each joint. Don't cut all the way through the straw. Repeat for all other fingers.

Step 8

Tape the straws down to the cardstock fingers so the notches line up with the fold lines. The cut-out notches should face up. Trim any excess straw length from the bottom. Straws should end in the palm area.

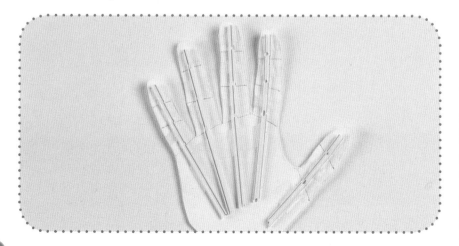

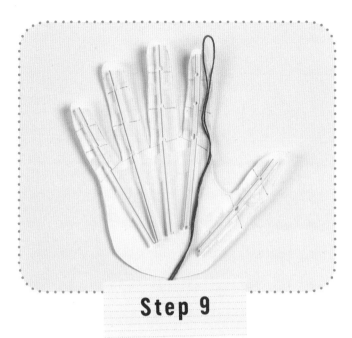

Step 9

Cut a piece of string or embroidery floss for each finger that is at least twice the length of the straw.

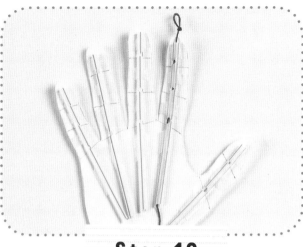

Step 10

Tie a double or triple knot at one end of the string. Thread the other end of the string through the top of the straw (the fingertip) and out the bottom (near the palm).

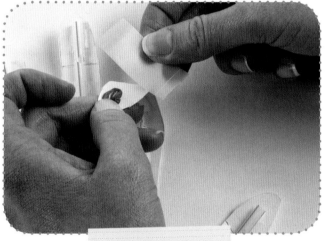

Step 11

Run the knotted end of the string up over the top of the fingertip and tape securely to the other side. Repeat for all fingers.

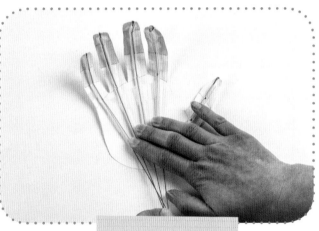

Step 12

Your artificial hand is now complete. *What happens when you pull the string at the bottom of a straw? Can you pull all strings at the same time? How is your artificial hand different from your real hand? How would you improve the design?*

HOW DOES IT WORK?

The human hand is an amazing work of engineering. It has five fingers that each have multiple joints. These joints are controlled by muscles and tendons. The muscles pull on the tendons, which pull on the joints and make them bend. Think about all of the ways your fingers bend. In your artificial hand, the notches in the straws act as the joints and the strings running through the straws act as the tendons.

FINGERPRINTS

Each person's fingerprints are unique. In investigations, a person might have their fingerprints tested to see if they are a match for fingerprints left at the crime scene. You can do a low tech version of dusting for fingerprints and recording them!

MATERIALS

- Clean glass
- A fine, powdery material such as flour or cocoa powder
- A brush
- Clear tape
- Dark paper
- White paper
- Pencil

Step 1

Press your finger against the clean glass to leave a fingerprint. It may help to rub your fingers together to bring oil to the surface. (You don't want to try this experiment right after washing your hands.)

Step 2

Hold the glass to the light to see if you've left a clear fingerprint. If not, try again.

Step 3

Use clear tape to "lift" the fingerprint from the glass. Press the tape to the glass, and remove it from the glass, slowly and carefully. It will be easiest to see against a dark background like black construction paper.

Step 5

Press a finger into the graphite left behind by the pencil.

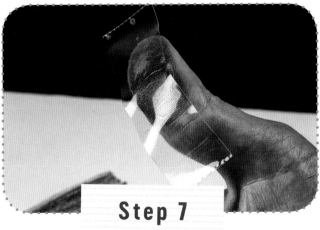

Step 7

Press tape against your finger and remove it. Perform this step slowly and carefully.

Step 4

Now record your own fingerprint. Scribble a square on a paper with a pencil.

Step 6

You'll end up with a lot of graphite on your finger!

Step 8

Compare the fingerprint lifted from an object against the fingerprint taken from graphite. Are they a match?

VISION

Vision varies tremendously in the animal world. Humans have binocular vision—each eye perceives an image, and our brain puts it together. If you close one eye, your depth perception can suffer. That is, it gets harder to figure out how far away something is.

Humans can see light in the visible spectrum. But some animals can see longer or shorter wavelengths than humans can.

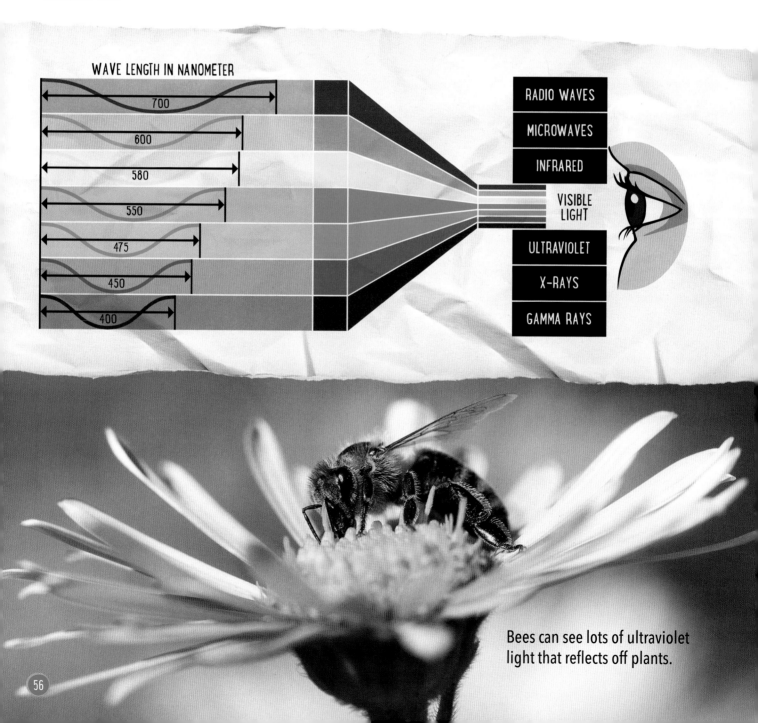

WAVE LENGTH IN NANOMETER

700
600
580
550
475
450
400

RADIO WAVES

MICROWAVES

INFRARED

VISIBLE LIGHT

ULTRAVIOLET

X-RAYS

GAMMA RAYS

Bees can see lots of ultraviolet light that reflects off plants.

Some snakes can see into the infrared spectrum. This helps them detect warm-blooded prey around them.

Night vision goggles rely on infrared energy, which gives off heat.

In humans, light enters the eyes through the pupil. The iris, the colored part of the eye, controls the size of the pupil and how much light gets into the eye. Light lands on the back of the eye, the retina, which has structures called rods and cones. Rods help us see in dim light, while cones help us see color. The optic nerve carries images to the brain for interpretation.

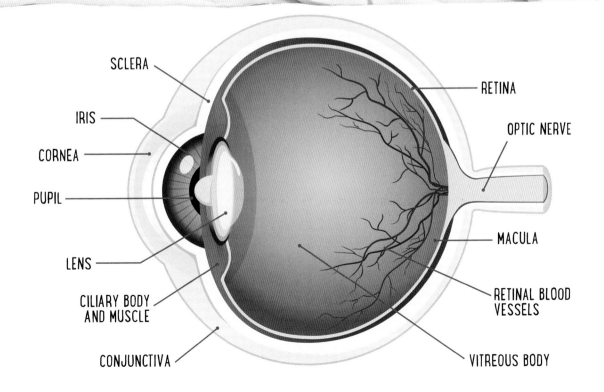

SCLERA

IRIS

CORNEA

PUPIL

LENS

CILIARY BODY
AND MUSCLE

CONJUNCTIVA

RETINA

OPTIC NERVE

MACULA

RETINAL BLOOD
VESSELS

VITREOUS BODY

CORNER OF YOUR EYE

You can see things around you without moving your head or your eyes! This is called peripheral vision. You can test the limits of this vision. It takes two people to do this activity, so grab a friend.

MATERIALS

- 1 black marker
- 4 other markers of different colors
- 5 index cards
- 6 popsicle sticks (pencils also work)
- Masking or painter's tape
- A table or desk
- A chair

Setting up:

1. On one index card, draw a small black dot.

2. Draw on each of the other cards a different shape in a different color.

3. Tape one card to each popsicle stick.

Experiment:

1. Sit at the table or desk. Hold the card with the black dot in one hand straight out in front of you.

2. Ask your friend to mix up the shape cards where you can't see.

3. Your friend puts one of the shape cards in your other hand without you looking at it.

4. Stare at the black dot in front of you. Keep your eyes on it the whole time. Do not move your head.

5. Hold the shape card straight out beside you. Slowly move it in an arc toward the black dot card. Remember: Don't look at it!

6. When you can see movement in the corner of your eye, stop your arm. Your friend puts a piece of tape on the table to mark that spot. Then continue slowly moving.

7. Stop so your friend can add a mark when you can tell what color the card is. Do the same for when you know what shape it is.

8. Do the same thing with the remaining three cards.

What do you see first? Last?

How far does your peripheral vision go?

EXTRA CHALLENGE!

Switch hands. The moving hand now holds the black dot. Your other hand moves with a shape card.

OPTICAL ILLUSIONS

Sometimes, you can trick your eyes and your brain.

Line Lengths

Which line is longer—the horizontal line or the vertical line?

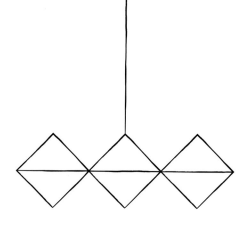

Heart and Soul

What color is the heart in each quadrant?

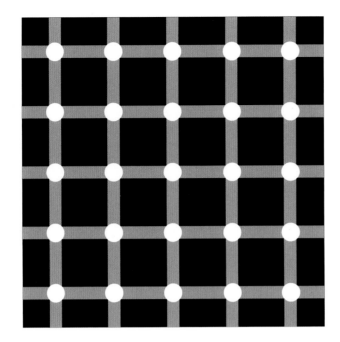

C

Deceptive Dots

If you let your eyes roam around this image, you're likely to experience a warping effect.

D

Flashing Dots

Stare at this grid long enough and the dots will flash on and off. Why?

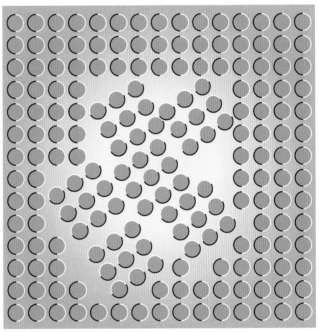

A. Though it may be hard to believe, the horizontal and vertical lines are equal length. The diamonds placed at the ends of the vertical line make it appear longer. The 3 diamonds laying over the horizontal line break this line. The interruption makes the combined parts seem shorter.

B. The pink hearts in the top right and bottom left squares are darker than the other 2 hearts, right? Wrong! All 4 hearts are identical in color. The lighter background color in the top right and bottom left squares make the pink hearts seem darker by contrast.

C. This is an afterimage illusion and a contrast illusion. The white dots look brighter because they are surrounded by a lot of black. This enhances the afterimage illusion, where an image of something stays in your eye even after you've looked away (like "seeing" a camera flash after it's already gone off).

D. This is known as anomalous motion, a term used to define the appearance of motion in a static image. Color contrasts and eye movement contribute to relative motion effects.

BLINKING

Blinking helps keep your eyes from getting dry. How often do you usually blink? How long can you go without blinking?

For this experiment, you'll need another person to help out, as well as a stopwatch or timer.

Step 1

Watch the other person for one minute. They should not try to keep from blinking, just blink naturally. How many times do they blink in one minute?

Step 2

Now, have that person watch you for one minute. How many times do you blink? Generally, people blink 10-15 times a minute, though they may blink less if they're concentrating on something.

Step 3

Run the experiment again. This time, try not to blink. How long can you keep from blinking?

Step 4

How long can the other person keep from blinking?

NOTES

Written by Adam Parrilli
Photo styling by Nick LaShure and Nicole Sulgit
Photography by Christopher Hiltz, Nick LaShure and Nicole Sulgit
Additional images from Shutterstock.com

First printing
Manufactured in China.
03/2021 Guangdong

8 7 6 5 4 3 2 1

SAFETY WARNING
All of the experiments and activities in this book MUST be performed with adult supervision. All projects contain a degree of risk, so carefully read all instructions before you begin and make sure that you have safety materials such as goggles, gloves, etc. Also make sure that you have safety equipment, such as a fire extinguisher and first aid kit, on hand. You are assuming the risk of any injury by conducting these activities and experiments. Publications International, Ltd. will not be liable for any injury or property damage.

Let's get social!
[instagram] @Publications_International
[facebook] @PublicationsInternational
[facebook] @BrainGames.TM
www.pilbooks.com

CONTENTS

26

30

60

INTRODUCTION

What does art have to do with other STEM topics? Plenty! Here are just some examples of the way art works with science, technology, engineering, and math.

Artists have looked to nature for inspiration and color palettes. They have also used objects from nature to make art. Artists used natural pigments and paints to create their artwork. Later, paints involved chemical mixtures.

Cooks and bakers use chemistry to make food that's tasty. But chefs also try to make food look good. Some food can be edible art!

When people design technology such as smartphones or TVs, they want it to work. They also want customers to like how it looks. People put a lot of thought into the artistic design of smartphones to make them easy to use and attractive. People who code video games spend time on the art, which helps tell the story.

Engineers and architects work together to make buildings and bridges that are both functional and pleasing to the eye.

Artists use math! They measure in order to get perspective right. They use geometry as they work with 3-D shapes.

Music is a kind of art too. Music uses sound energy to create arrangements of sounds that we like to listen to.

In this book, you'll learn more about color theory, art history, and music.

WHAT IS PAPER?

Paper was invented more than 2,000 years ago in ancient China. It is most commonly used for writing, drawing, packaging, and printing. Without paper we wouldn't have books, newspapers, magazines, or paper money.

WHAT CAME BEFORE PAPER?

Before paper was created, cave drawings were used to communicate. Other methods used to reach out to others were smoke signals and drums. In ancient Egypt, they made a kind of paper from the papyrus plant. Papyrus is where the word paper comes from.

WHAT IS PAPER MADE OF?

Did you know that the paper you write on every day is generally made from trees? Paper can be made from flax, cotton, and hemp, among other plant fibers, but mostly it is made from logs or from recycled paper that itself was made from logs.

HOW IS PAPER MADE?

Let's explore the process of making paper. It all gets started with the cutting down of trees. The trees are then sent, in log form, to a paper factory, or mill. The bark must be peeled from the trees. Then the wood is chopped into very small pieces. These wood pieces are boiled with water and a few other chemicals until they turn into a slushy, mushy pulp.

The pulp is then poured through a strainer to separate the pulp from the liquid. The thick pulp is then squeezed between felt-covered press rollers to absorb extra water. This pulp mat now passes through hot rollers, as many times as necessary, until it is completely dry. Once it's fully dried, the paper is ready. It comes in roll form, much like the way you see toilet paper or paper towels at home. Paper can also be output in huge sheets.

MAKE YOUR OWN PATTERNED PAPER

You can buy pretty patterned stationery, or create your own with just water and food coloring.

MATERIALS

- Food coloring
- Squeeze or spray bottles
- Paper (absorbent, textured paper works best)
- Paper towels
- Newspaper or an old sheet

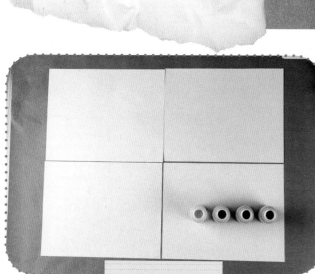

Step 1

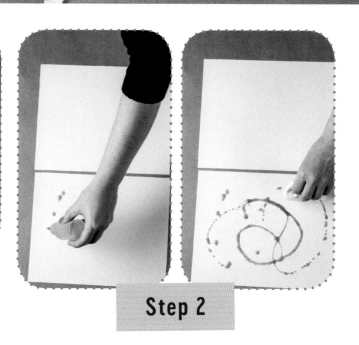

Step 2

Lay out the sheets of paper you want to decorate. This can get messy, so it's best to have them on a surface that can be cleaned easily, or put down an old sheet or newspapers. Fill the bottles with water and a few drops of food coloring.

Spray or spritz the paper with the colorful water.

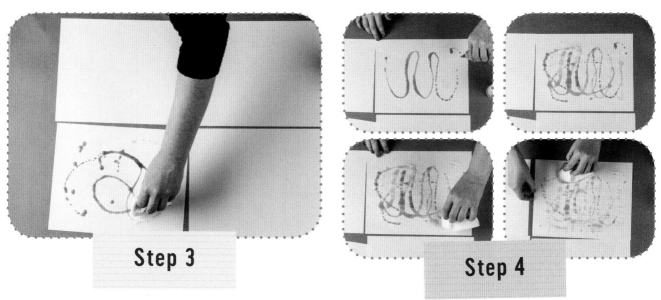

Step 3

Gently blot extra water away with a paper towel.

Step 4

You can mix colors!

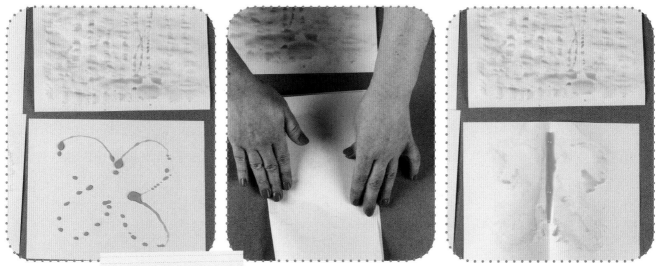

Step 5

For symmetrical designs, you can fold the paper in half.

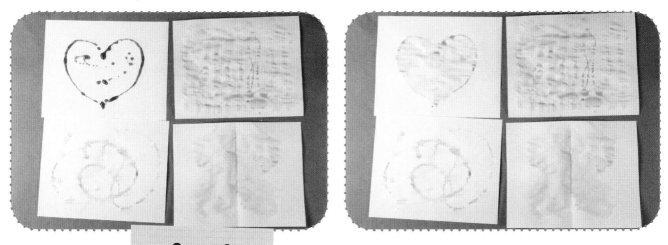

Step 6

Leave your designs overnight to dry.

JUMPING FROG

Make a frog that jumps with just a sheet of 3" by 3" paper. Press down on the frog's back and it will hop!

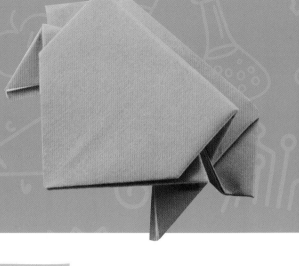

Step 1

Position your paper as a square, with the blank side facing up.

Step 2

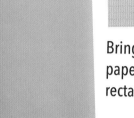

Bring the left side of the paper over to make a rectangle.

Step 3

Bring the top left corner of the rectangle over to the right edge of the paper.

Step 4

Unfold to see the crease you just created.

Step 5

Do the same with the right corner.

Step 6

Flip the paper over. Bring the top of the paper down and create a fold. The fold should cross the intersection of your two diagonal creases.

Step 7

Then unfold to see the crease you just created and flip the paper over again.

Step 8

Touch the center point as shown in the picture, and then bring in the sides to create a triangular shape.

Step 9

Bring up the bottom half of the model to the bottom of the triangle.

Step 10

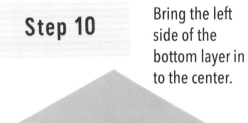

Bring the left side of the bottom layer in to the center.

Step 11

Do the same on the right.

Step 12

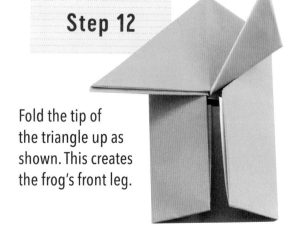

Fold the tip of the triangle up as shown. This creates the frog's front leg.

Step 13

Do the same on the other side.

Step 14

Fold the top layer of the bottom right corner of the model as shown. Do the same on the other side.

Step 15

Fold the frog in half, bringing the top layer down to the bottom corner.

Step 16

Flip the frog over so that you're seeing the square of its back.

Step 17

Bring the bottom of the square back and fold it in half.

Step 18

Press down on the base of the frog's back and release to make it hop away!

ORIGAMI PINWHEEL

Step 1

Position your paper with the color/pattern facing up.

Step 2

Fold from left to right and then open the paper. Fold from the top to the bottom and open the paper.

Step 3

Create two more folds along the diagonal lines. Open the paper; you should see the fold lines as shown in the picture.

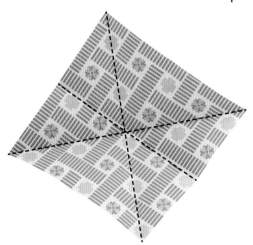

Step 4

Bring one corner of the paper in to the center of the paper.

Step 5 Do the same with the other three corners.

Step 6 Open the paper back up.

Step 7 Flip it over.

Step 8 Fold each edge to the center line, then unfold the paper.

14

Step 9

Do the same with the opposite edges. Then unfold the paper.

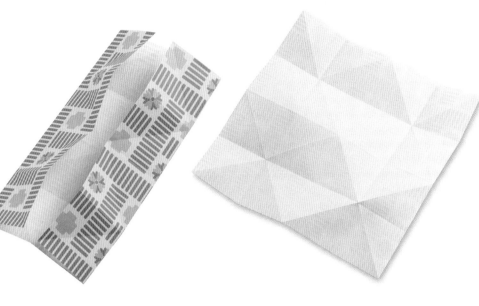

Step 10

Fold over two edges as shown, leaving the corner out.

Step 11

Now flatten the corner as shown.

Step 12

Moving clockwise, do the same for the next corner.

Step 13

The last two folds will be flattened in one step.

SUN AND PAPER

Use the power of the Sun to create patterns on your paper.

MATERIALS

- Dark construction paper
- Rocks or other heavy objects
- Pretty leaves
- Clear plastic wrap

Step 1

On a sunny day, lay out pretty leaves on top of construction paper.

Step 2

Place a sheet of plastic wrap over the paper and leaves.

Step 3

Weigh down the plastic wrap and paper with rocks or other small heavy objects. Let the Sun do its work!

Step 4

Over time, the Sun's solar energy lightens the paper it can reach. Furniture in sunny windows often fades over time because of Sun exposure, too.

Step 5

Remove the leaves. You have used solar energy to create a piece of art!

THE COLOR WHEEL

PRIMARY COLORS

The primary colors are red, yellow, and blue. When we say primary colors, what we mean is that these three colors are the source of all other colors. Primary colors cannot be mixed or created from other colors. What do you think is the most popular color in the world? The answer is blue.

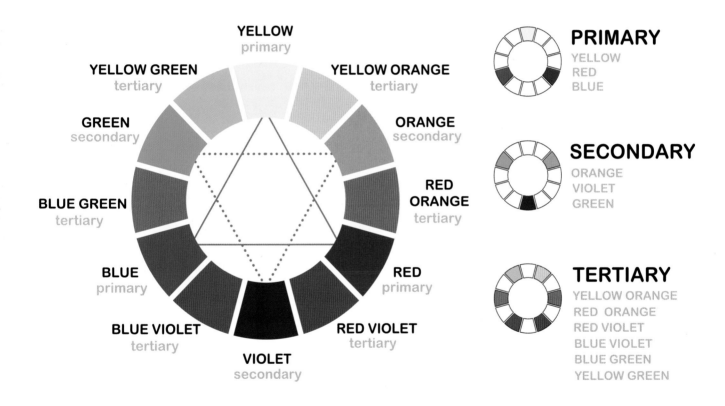

PRIMARY
YELLOW
RED
BLUE

SECONDARY
ORANGE
VIOLET
GREEN

TERTIARY
YELLOW ORANGE
RED ORANGE
RED VIOLET
BLUE VIOLET
BLUE GREEN
YELLOW GREEN

SECONDARY COLORS

The secondary colors are orange, green, and purple. Secondary colors are made by mixing two of the primary colors. The way to make each of these colors specifically is: blue and yellow make green, yellow and red make orange, and red and blue make purple. What's neat is that the amount of each color you use when mixing the primary colors produces a different shade of the secondary color. Amounts matter! If you add more red than yellow to a red-yellow mix, you get a reddish-orange, and if you add more yellow than red, you get a yellowish-orange.

COMPLEMENTARY COLORS

Complementary colors are any two colors that are directly opposite each other on the color wheel, for example, red and green. For each of the three secondary colors, their complementary color is the one primary color that was not used to create it. So, for orange, it's blue and for purple, it's yellow. If you want to make a color really stick out, try placing complementary colors next to each other. This visually intensifies both colors!

Florists often use flowers of complementary colors as they create a bouquet.

When white light enters a prism, it breaks into its separate colors. Basically, the glass causes the light to bend. Since each color travels at a different speed, it bends a different amount, producing a rainbow effect.

PRIMARY AND SECONDARY COLORS

Let's say you want your food to be orange, green, and purple, but you only have red, yellow, and blue food coloring. No problem!

MATERIALS

- Three glasses
- Red, yellow, and blue food coloring
- Water

Step 1

Fill three glasses with water.

Step 2

Add a few drops of red food coloring to the first glass.

Step 3

Add a few drops of yellow food coloring.

Step 4

Stir the food coloring into the water. Red and yellow make orange!

Step 5

Add a few drops of yellow food coloring to the second glass.

Step 6

Add a few drops of blue food coloring to the second glass.

Step 7

Stir the food coloring into the water. Yellow and blue make green!

Step 8

Add a few drops of red food coloring to the last glass.

Step 9

Now add a few drops of blue food coloring.

Step 10

Red and blue make purple!

COLORFUL CANDY

Create a pretty pattern with candy and water!

MATERIALS

- Small, shallow dish
- Hard-shelled candy such as M&Ms
- Water

Step 1

Pour water into the dish.

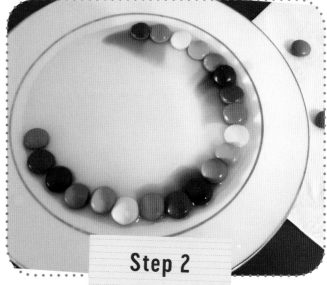

Step 2

Line the dish with candy.

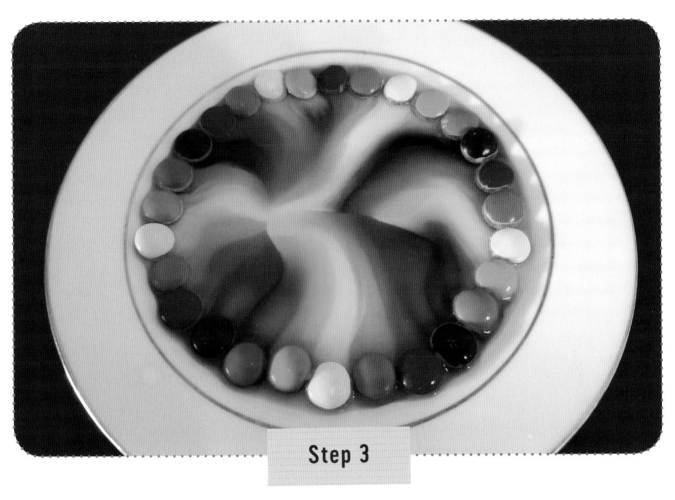

Step 3

The water leaches out the dye in the candy shell.

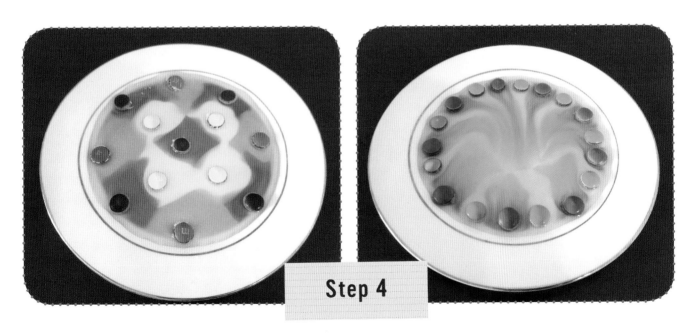

Step 4

Create different patterns using your favorite colors!

PIGMENTS

WHAT IS A PIGMENT?

A pigment is a powdered substance that is used to give something color. When a pigment is added to a liquid, it gives color to things like paints or inks. Pigments can be natural (from the Earth) or man-made. Natural pigments can come from animals, plants, rocks, and minerals.

ROCK AND MINERAL PIGMENTS

Making paints from rocks or minerals is relatively easy. The rocks or minerals will be the pigments and need to be broken into small pieces, perhaps with a hammer. Then they will need to be crushed into a fine powder. Finally, paints are created by mixing the pigment with different liquid additives. This will depend on what type of paint you wish to make. There are oil paints, pastels, acrylic paints, watercolor paints, and tempera, which actually uses an egg yolk!

PLANT PIGMENTS

Plants can also be used as pigments. Two popular varieties are the indigo plant, which produces a beautiful blue, and the madder plant, which produces both red and pink. Traditionally, the madder plant's roots were dried in the sun and then pounded to produce an orange powder.

ANIMAL PIGMENTS

Animals, though not as common as plants or minerals, are sometimes used for pigments. Certain cochineal insects that live on cactus plants can be dried and ground to produce red powder. The color Tyrian purple requires thousands of tiny snails to make a rich shade of purple. Tyrian purple was highly valued in ancient Rome, so much so that it was referred to as "royal purple."

POISONOUS PAINTS

History has shown us that some paints are poisonous. The most famous one is probably white lead. This dangerous paint was banned in the 1970s. Scheele's green and Paris green were much more vibrant than natural greens, but these pigments were extremely toxic and later used as insecticides. Lastly, there was uranium orange, which was used to color ceramics and glass. Plates painted with uranium orange should definitely not be eaten off of!

PAINTING WITH
CHLOROPHYLL

Spinach is great for your health, filled with nutrients. In a pinch, it can also be used when you need green pigment.

- Spinach
- Metal spoon
- Paper

Step 1

Place the spinach on your paper where you would like the green to show up.

Step 2

Fold the paper in half, over the spinach. Press the paper with a spoon to release the green pigment in it, the chlorophyll that gives spinach its green color. It leaves a green residue on the page.

Step 3

For a further release of green pigment, you can also crumple up a bunch of spinach in your hands and rub it against the paper.

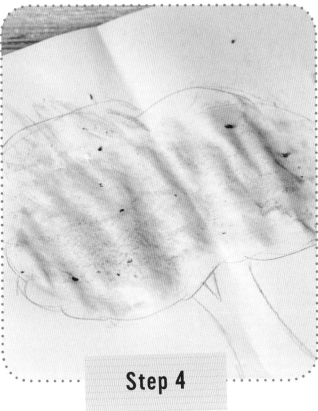

Step 4

Voilà, you've added green to your painting!

PAINTING WITH BERRIES

Berries provide natural red or purple pigments.

MATERIALS

- Blackberries, raspberries, or both. You can try other types of berries as well.
- A bowl for each kind of berry you're using
- A bowl for eggs
- Egg(s)
- Paper
- Paintbrush(es)
- A strainer
- A fork and a spoon
- Paper towels

Step 1

Place the berries you're going to use in the strainer, above a bowl of about the same size.

Step 2

Mash the berries with the fork.

Step 3

Colorful juice falls into the bowl.

Step 4

For extra shine, crack an egg into a separate bowl.

Step 5

Mix the egg in with your paint.

Step 6

Gather your paintbrush and paper. This can be messy and the paint can soak through the paper, so placing a paper towel underneath your paper is recommended on fabric surfaces or ones that are difficult to wipe down.

Step 7

Start painting!

Raspberry juice provides a lighter red pigment.

POLISHED ROCKS

You can decorate beautiful swirling patterns on rocks with just nail polish!

MATERIALS

- Nail polish in different colors
- Gloves
- Toothpicks
- Bowls (paper bowls work best and can be thrown out after)
- Rocks

Step 1

Fill a bowl or bowls with water. Add a few drops of nail polish.

Step 2

Add a few drops of nail polish in a different color. Add as many colors as you would like.

Step 3

Swirl the nail polish with a toothpick.

Step 4

Swirl your rock through the water and nail polish.

Step 5

The nail polish will leave a thin coating.

Step 6

Set your rock aside to dry.

Step 7

Create as many color combinations as you would like.

WHY DOES IT WORK?

Nail polish, like oil, does not mix with water. Instead, it forms a thin film on top of the water that adheres to the rock.

PERSPECTIVE

Perspective is a technique artists use to represent three dimensional objects (like you and me) on a two dimensional surface (a piece of paper or canvas). A good use of perspective will create an illusion of both depth and space in a work of art. The same rules of perspective apply whether the work is a landscape, still life, portrait, or figure painting.

PERSPECTIVE VOCABULARY

Before going into further detail on a few types of perspective, an explanation of a few terms will be helpful. First, there is the horizon line, which is an eye-level line the artist places horizontally across the surface of the picture. Parallel lines or orthogonals are two or more diagonal lines that converge and meet at the vanishing point on the horizon line. The vanishing point, as you may have guessed, is a point where all the parallel lines seem to meet and gradually disappear.

ONE-POINT PERSPECTIVE

One-point perspective has one vanishing point at the horizon line. Using one-point perspective adds more depth to an image. This type of perspective can easily be used to portray things such as railroad tracks, highways, roads, hallways, or room interiors.

TWO-POINT PERSPECTIVE

Two-point perspective contains two vanishing points on the horizon line and gives a very realistic feel to the work of art. Also known as three-quarter perspective or angular perspective, this view is often used to show something like the corner of a building on a street, or a group of buildings.

ATMOSPHERIC PERSPECTIVE

The last type of perspective we'll cover is atmospheric perspective. This perspective is also used to create the illusion of depth, but uses color rather than horizon lines and vanishing points. Objects that are further away have blurry edges and appear lighter in color.

ONE-POINT PERSPECTIVE

Draw a picture with a vanishing point and a horizon.

Step 1

Draw two diagonal lines. Each one should start at one corner and go to the opposite corner. The point where they meet represents the vanishing point.

Step 2

Draw a horizontal line that intersects with your vanishing point. This is your horizon.

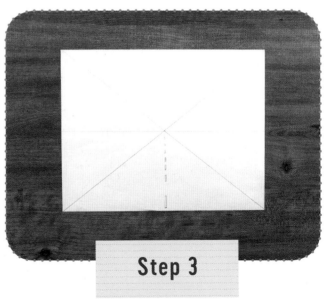

Step 3

Let's make the area at the bottom into a road. Draw lane markers on the road. The further away they are, the smaller they appear to be.

Step 4

Draw a vertical line from the vanishing point to the end of the page. The tops of your telephone poles will intersect with that line, so that they appear to grow smaller when they are further away.

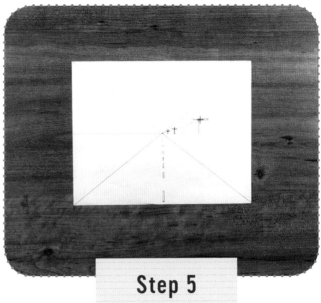

Step 5

Draw in your other telephone poles.

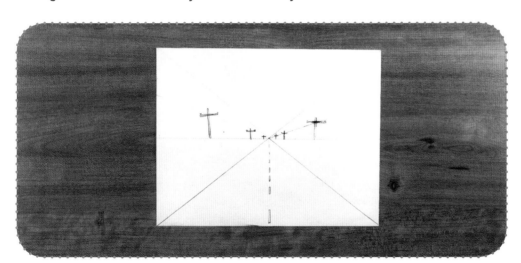

Step 6

Draw in telephone poles along the other side.

Step 7

Color in your picture and erase any reference lines you don't need. How closely can you get your picture to match this photograph?

TWO-POINT PERSPECTIVE

Use the techniques of two-point perspective to create a simple box that looks three-dimensional.

Step 1

Draw a horizontal line across your index card. Mark each end to indicate a vanishing point.

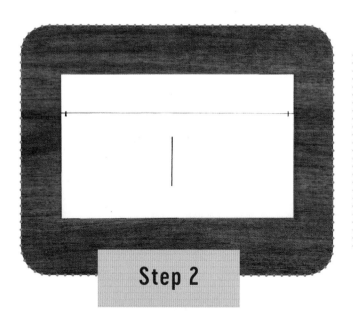

Step 2

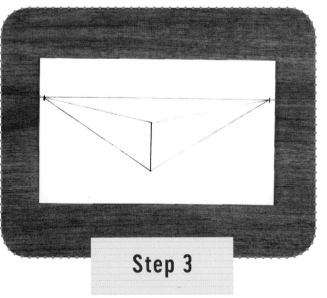

Step 3

Draw a vertical line slightly below the horizontal line. This is one visible edge of your box.

Draw light lines from each vanishing point to the top and bottom of the vertical line.

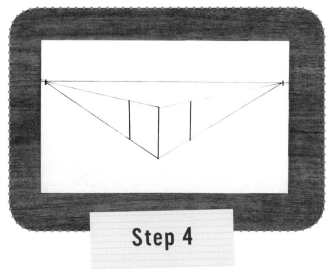

Step 4

Draw two vertical lines to represent two more edges of the box.

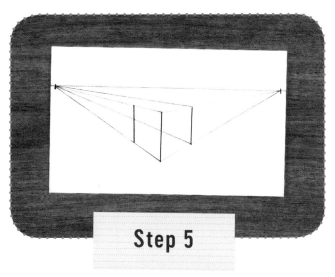

Step 5

Draw two light lines from the vanishing point on the left, to the top and bottom of the vertical line on the right.

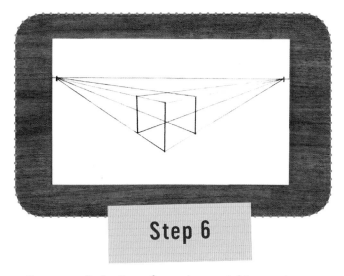

Step 6

Draw two light lines from the vanishing point on the right, to the top and bottom of the vertical line on the left.

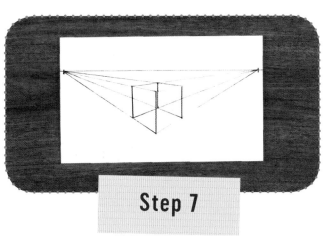

Step 7

Draw a vertical line to represent the final edge of the box.

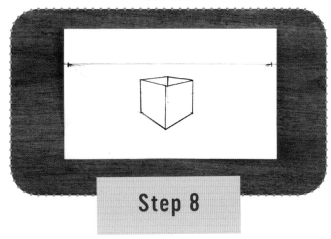

Step 8

For an open box, erase any extra lines that you don't need.

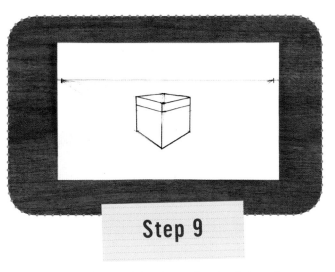

Step 9

For a closed box, add in lines for the lid and erase completely the line you drew in step 7.

COMPOSITION AND SPACE IN A PAINTING

When talking about space within a piece of art, we are referring to the background, foreground, and middle ground. Space also includes the areas found around, between, and within the forms, shapes, colors, and lines that make up the work of art. The concepts of positive and negative space are abstract, meaning they are not something you can touch or feel.

NEGATIVE AND POSITIVE SPACE

Negative space is the space surrounding an object, figure, or form. Positive space refers to the object, figure, or form itself that resides within the negative space. Understanding these two terms will make it easier for you to create pieces of art that display greater balance and depth.

HAND EXERCISE

Imagine or try this out for yourself. Place your non-writing hand stretched out on a piece of paper and carefully trace around each of your fingers. Now, color in the areas between your fingers and around your hand. As you lift your hand up, you will see that by coloring in the space surrounding your hand, you have actually created an image of your hand's shape. In this example, the negative space is the colored area or space surrounding your hand. And the positive space is the image of your hand itself.

USE OF SPACE

As a general rule, an object in the background is considered negative space. As you look at more and more pieces of art, the negative space may be just as important to an artist's concept as the object occupying the positive space. It could very well be the artist's intention to use negative space to convey a deeper meaning and get you thinking about what they are trying to tell you with their art.

REALISM

THE ORIGIN OF REALISM

Realism (also known as naturalism) began in France in the late 1840s, following the French Revolution. It took until the 1860s for realism to catch on here in America. The style used simple, basic detail unlike the pretty and imaginative detail of previous styles of art. Realism is considered the first modern art movement.

REALIST TECHNIQUE

Realist painters often used natural brushstrokes and rough paint texture to portray their everyday subjects. Just because the artists were painting people and places realistically does not mean that it was easy to do. In fact, you could argue that realist paintings were more difficult because the audience was so familiar with the subjects being painted. Realism was known for its very high level of detail and clarity.

WHAT COMES NEXT?

Impressionism (which we will talk about next) appeared in France in the 1860s, and by the 1880s, the realism movement had ended. Although it may have fallen out of style, realism has never really gone away.

"A Burial at Ornans" by Gustave Courbet is an example of a realist painting. The scene depicts the burial of the painter's great uncle. The people in the painting are the ones that were actually there, not models, all real, like the realism movement.

Jean-Francois Millet's "Woman with a Rake" from 1857 was later copied by Vincent van Gogh. Millet's work showed an everyday task and fit right in with other realist paintings.

"A Wagon of the Third Class" by Honore Daumier is a realist painting depicting a humble, seemingly fatherless family as they travel. Notice how weary they look. Daumier completed this painting between 1862 and 1864.

THE GRID TECHNIQUE

The grid technique helps you create detailed drawings, one square at a time. Focus on one square in the image on the left page, then recreate that image in the square with the matching coordinates on the right page.

	A	B	C	D	E	F	G	H	I	J	K	L	M	
1														1
2														2
3														3
4														4
5														5
6														6
7														7
8														8
9														9
10														10
11														11
12														12
13														13
14														14
15														15
16														16
	A	B	C	D	E	F	G	H	I	J	K	L	M	

IMPRESSIONISM

Impressionism was an art movement that started in France in the late 1860s. The impressionists were not looking to paint a realistic picture; rather an impression of what a person, object, or landscape looked like to them. They wanted to capture a moment in time as it was happening, before it passed them by.

Vincent van Gogh's "The Starry Night"

IMPRESSIONIST SUBJECTS

Much like realism, the subject matter of impressionist art focused on ordinary, everyday people, places, and things. Some of the works showed things like ballet dancers doing exercises, a waitress in a restaurant, horses getting ready for a race, or even scenes of people cooking, sleeping, and bathing.

EN PLEIN AIR

The impressionists often painted outdoors, or "in the open air." Their goal was to observe and paint the effects of sunlight and color as they changed throughout the day. Impressionist paintings tend to show a broad, rapid style, with brushstrokes that are easily seen and colors that are usually bright.

ON REPEAT

Impressionists sometimes painted the same view or subject over and over trying to capture different moments in light, color, and time. French painter Claude Monet produced a twenty-five canvas series of paintings featuring haystacks. The series is known for its use of repetition to show differences in light across various times of day, seasons, and types of weather.

PUBLIC REACTION TO IMPRESSIONISM

Many people didn't like impressionism as they thought it was a bit messy and felt that the paintings looked unfinished. Some critics believed the impressionists couldn't draw and their compositions were strange. Of course, there were plenty of admirers of impressionist art as well.

Eventually the impressionist style spread to many countries across Europe, to North America and Australia. Some artists continued to paint in the impressionist style throughout the 20th century.

Monet's "Impression, Sunrise" (below left) is the painting that gave birth to the name of the movement, impressionism, as given by a critic. The painting hangs at the Musée Marmottan Monet in Paris, France. "Impression, Sunrise" was stolen in 1985, but was recovered undamaged in 1990.

"Paris Street; Rainy Day" (below middle) is a famous impressionist work by Gustave Caillebotte from 1877. Notice how the foreground is in focus, while the background becomes more and more blurry.

Renoir's "Dance at Moulin de la Galette" from 1876 (below right) is one of impressionism's most highly revered masterpieces. On display at the Musée d'Orsay in Paris, France, the painting shows a typical Sunday gathering of Parisians for food and drink.

POINTILLISM

Pointillism was a completely different method of painting. Rather than use brushstrokes that flowed, a pointillist painter would apply small dots of color to a surface so that from a distance they blended together.

ORIGINS OF POINTILLISM

Created in 1886 by George Seurat and Paul Signac in Paris, France, pointillism was a scientific way of painting. Seurat actually preferred the term "divisionism," but pointillism is the name that stuck. The technique was completely at odds with the traditional method of mixing colors on a palette.

APPLICATIONS OF POINTILLISM

The many small dots placed close together work to trick your eye into mixing the colors and forming an image when looking at pointillist art. You might find it interesting to know that today's computer screens and televisions use pixels to form images just like the many dots of pointillism.

Vincent van Gogh painted many self-portraits. One of the most famous includes elements of pointillism. This 1887 piece called "Self-Portrait" (above, right) resides at the Art Institute of Chicago.

"The Pine Tree at San Tropez" (above) is a pointillist work by co-creator of the method, Paul Signac. The painting is on display at the Pushkin Museum in Moscow, Russia.

POINTILLISM IN PRACTICE

Make your own pointillist painting!

- Watercolor paints
- Water
- Cotton swabs
- Paper or index card

Step 1

Dampen a cotton swab very lightly. You don't want the paint to run. Dip it in your paint and make a dot on your paper.

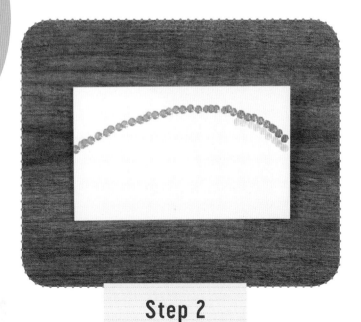

Step 2

Continue to make a picture with dots…

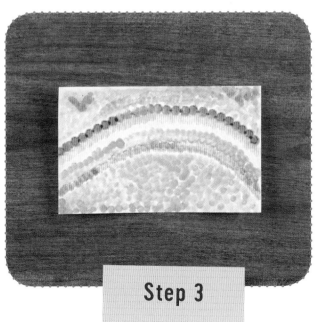

Step 3

…until you have a finished picture!

CUBISM

Cubism was a style of painting that started in the early 1900s. In cubism, the artist painted an object from lots of different angles all in the same picture. To depict three dimensions, they would break up the subject into many different shapes and then repaint it from various angles. The two artists who invented cubism were Pablo Picasso and Georges Braque. The name cubism came from an art critic that said one of Braque's paintings looked like it was made up of cubes. Some of the most common subjects in cubist art were people, musical instruments, bottles, glasses, and playing cards.

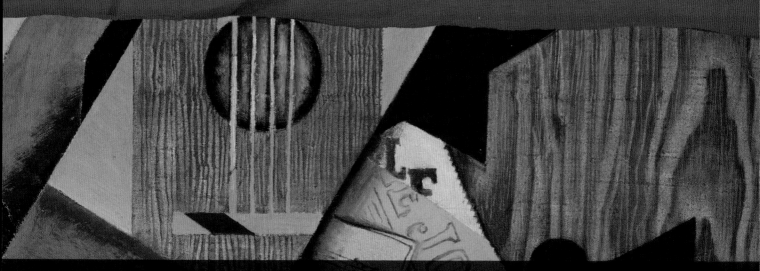

ANALYTICAL CUBISM

There were two different types of cubism. The first style ran from 1910 to 1912, and was called analytical cubism. These artists analyzed subjects and broke them down into multiple blocks. They then painted the different parts with overlapping planes, or rectangular shapes. The painters used very few colors because they wanted the viewer to focus on the shapes more than anything else.

SYNTHETIC CUBISM

The second type of cubism began in 1912 and was known as synthetic cubism. The artists that practiced this cubist style introduced other media to their paintings. They would glue colored paper, newspaper, or cloth onto the canvas to add texture. This is where we get the term collage from. In addition, synthetic cubism was much brighter and more colorful than analytical cubism.

THE END OF CUBISM

Cubism spread into other platforms as well. Picasso made cubist sculptures, and architects used cubist techniques in designing buildings. By 1919 the cubism movement had mostly come to an end, but like other movements, there are still cubist fans today.

Georges Braque's 1909 painting "Violin and Palette" is an example of analytical cubism. Braque used neutral browns and grays and attempted to show the same item from different points of view in this painting. Musical instruments appear frequently in Cubist paintings.

"Three Musicians" or "Musicians with Masks" is another notable cubist work by Pablo Picasso. It was painted in such a way to give the appearance of cut paper. "Three Musicians" emphasizes lively colors, angular shapes, and flat patterns.

ABSTRACT
EXPRESSIONISM

Abstract expressionism developed in New York City following World War II. Although it was not one cohesive style, abstract expressionist artists all strove to use abstraction (depicting forms not drawn from the visible world) to convey strong emotional content.

ACTION PAINTERS VS. COLOR FIELD PAINTERS

Within abstract expressionism there were two major types of artist: the action painters who attacked their canvases with expressive, spontaneous brushstrokes; and the color field painters who covered their canvases with large areas of a single color.

FAMOUS ABSTRACT EXPRESSIONISTS

Jackson Pollock was the best-known action painter. He painted with the canvas on the ground, pouring paint from the can, throwing it with a stick, or dripping it with a brush. Mark Rothko was famous for his color field painting style. He used large-scale canvases and painted soft-edged rectangular forms set within a colored field.

SPLATTER PAINTING

This is a funny, messy activity that you might want to do outdoors in old clothes. If you do it indoors, put down an old sheet or cloth beneath your poster board.

MATERIALS

- Poster board
- Plastic cutlery
- Acrylic or tempera paints. Add a little water so they will be runny and fluid.

Step 1

"Load" your spoon, knife, or fork with paint. With a flick of your wrist, paint sails onto your canvas.

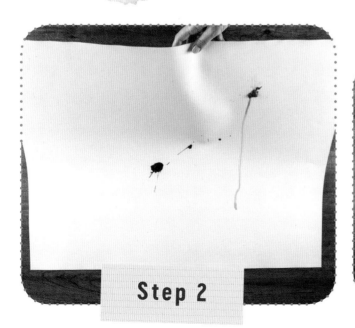

Step 2

You can also tilt it up to let the paint run.

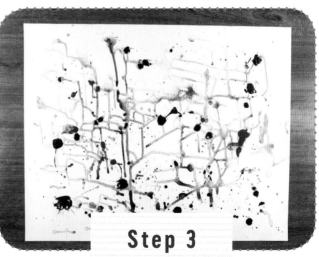

Step 3

Walk around your canvas as you work. Experiment with your paint textures by adding more water. Above all, have fun!

KINETIC ART

Kinetic art involves movement–for example, sculptures with pieces that are moved by the wind or by a motor.

Alexander Calder (1898-1976) was a prominent artist who made several mobiles and other kinetic sculptures. This piece is located in Paris.

Bucket Fountain, in New Zealand, incorporates water in its movement.

This sculpture by Tamara Kvesitadze is found in the country of Georgia.

David Czerny's sculpture, found in Prague, Czech Republic, depicts writer Franz Kafka.

CREATE YOUR OWN
KINETIC SCULPTURE

Can you use materials you have around the house to create a mobile or other kinetic sculpture that reacts to the wind?

SUGGESTED MATERIALS

- Tape
- Glue
- Craft dowels
- Ribbon
- Cardboard
- Paper
- Beads

Use a vase and craft dowels to create a kinetic sculpture bouquet! The beads and curled paper react to the wind.

Paper cups and construction paper can be used to create a simple, fun mobile.

MUSICAL INSTRUMENTS

Musical instruments have been around for a long time—flutes made of animal bones that date back 42,000 years have been found in Germany. Instruments are used for entertainment, rituals and religious services, and more. Music really is its own language and the many instruments can be used to convey countless different emotions.

The five major types of musical instruments are percussion, woodwind, stringed, brass, and keyboard.

PERCUSSION

Percussion instruments are typically hit or shaken. These include drums that are hit with sticks (or with the hands), as well as tambourines or maracas that are shaken.

WOODWINDS

Woodwind instruments are made of wood and metal and get their sound from a person blowing air into or across the mouthpiece. A flute or a piccolo produces sound by blowing air across the edge on the side of the instrument. The other type of woodwinds use a reed, or thin piece of wood, to create sound when air vibrates the reed. The clarinet and saxophone have one reed, and the oboe and bassoon have two reeds, or a double reed.

STRINGED

Stringed instruments make sound by the vibration of strings. A guitar is a stringed instrument whose sound comes from the plucking of the strings with one's hand, fingers, or a pick. Other similarly played instruments include the harp, banjo, lute, and sitar. Another set of stringed instruments are played by moving a bow across the strings. The main bowed instruments are the violin, cello, and double bass.

BRASS

Brass instruments include the trumpet, tuba, trombone, French horn, bugle, and cornet. These brass instruments, like the woodwinds, require a mouthpiece and wind power from the mouth to push air through the instrument to vibrate and make sound.

KEYBOARD

Keyboard instruments are played with the hands. Pianos, organs, and harpsichords are examples of keyboard instruments.

HARMONICA

Make your own harmonica and explore sound waves.
How can you make different sounds?

2 jumbo craft sticks

Wide rubber band

Plastic straw

Ruler

2 smaller rubber bands

Scissors

Step 1

Stretch the wide rubber band lengthwise over one of the craft sticks.

Step 2

Cut two pieces of straw, each 1–1½ inches (2½–3¾ cm) long.

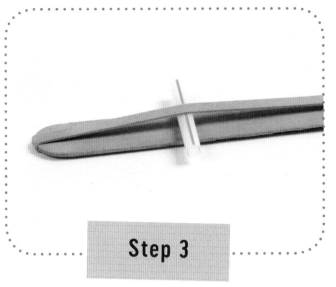

Step 3

Place one straw piece under the rubber band, about 2 inches (5 cm) from one end of the craft stick.

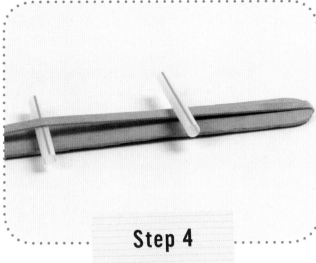

Step 4

Place the other straw piece on top of the rubber band, about 2 inches (5 cm) from the other end of the craft stick.

Step 5

Place the second craft stick on top of the first one, creating a sandwich with the straw pieces in the middle.

Step 6

Wrap a smaller rubber band about ½ inch (1¼ cm) from each end. To play your harmonica, put your mouth in the middle and blow through the sticks (not the straws). *Do you feel anything vibrating? Can you make different sounds by blowing through different areas, blowing harder or softer, or by moving the straws?*

HOW DOES IT WORK?

The sounds we hear are sound waves traveling through the air. Sound waves originate from a vibrating object, such as a vocal cord, and travel through the air. When you blow into your harmonica, you make the large rubber band vibrate, and that vibration produces sound. To change the pitch, slide the straws closer together or farther apart. When you slide the straws closer together, the section of rubber band that is vibrating is shorter, so it makes a higher sound.

MAKE YOUR OWN GUITAR

Rubber bands form the strings on this DIY guitar.

MATERIALS

- Shoebox
- Paper towel tube
- Glue
- Scissors
- Rubber bands of varying thickness
- Compass

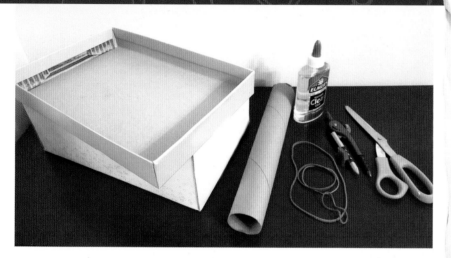

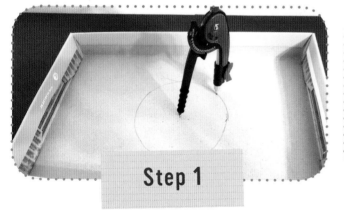

Step 1

Using the compass, draw a circle in the center of the lid of the shoebox.

Step 2

Ask an adult to score the circle with the tip of one blade of the scissors.

Step 3

Remove the circle from the shoebox lid. From it, cut out two narrow strips.

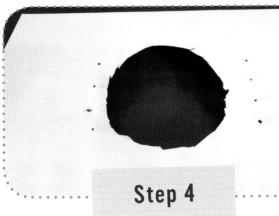

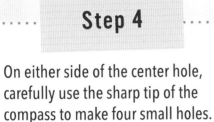

Step 4

On either side of the center hole, carefully use the sharp tip of the compass to make four small holes.

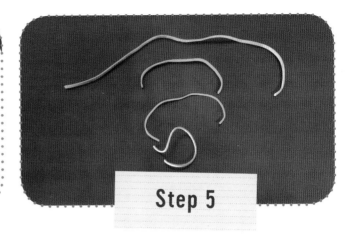

Step 5

Cut each rubber band to make your strings.

Step 6

Thread the rubber bands through the holes.

Step 7

Tape down the rubber bands to the inside of the box.

Step 8

Glue down the strips of cardboard from step 3 to help keep the strings taut and in place.

Step 9

Draw a circle around the cardboard tube on one end of the box and cut it out.

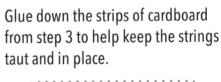

Step 10

Fit the cardboard tube into the hole.

Step 11

Place the lid on the box and try out your guitar!

WATER GLASS XYLOPHONE

Create a symphony with water, glasses, and a spoon!

Step 1

Leave one glass empty. Fill the glass next to it with ¼ cup of water.

Step 2

Pour ½ cup in the third glass.

Step 3

Continue pouring water in each glass, increasing the amount by ¼ cup each time.

Glass 1: empty
Glass 2: ¼ cup
Glass 3: ½ cup
Glass 4: ¾ cup
Glass 5: 1 cup
Glass 6: 1 ¼ cup
Glass 7: 1 ½ cup
Glass 8: 1 ¾ cup

Step 4

Fill the glasses with different colors of food coloring if you'd like.

Step 5

Tap the glasses with the spoon to play a melody!

FOR FURTHER FUN

Try using spoons made of different materials. What material produces the best result? Pour the same amount of water in a short wide glass, a short thin glass, a tall wide glass, and a tall skinny glass. Do they produce the same pitch?

STRAW PIPES

Create your own set of colorful panpipes with straws.

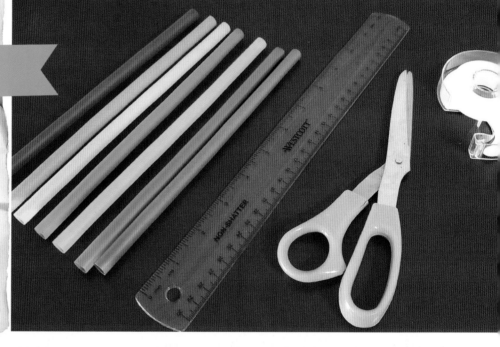

MATERIALS

- 7 milkshake straws
- Clear tape
- Ruler
- Scissors

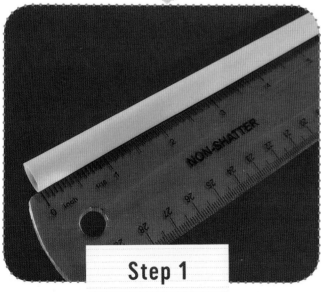

Step 1

Leave one straw at full length. Cut an inch off the second straw.

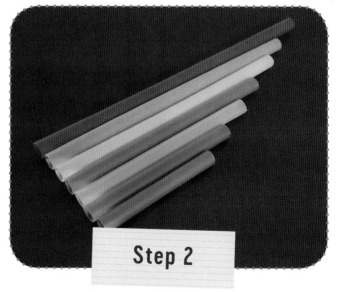

Step 2

Cut two inches off the third straw, three inches off the fourth straw, and so forth, until you have seven straws that vary by one inch in length.

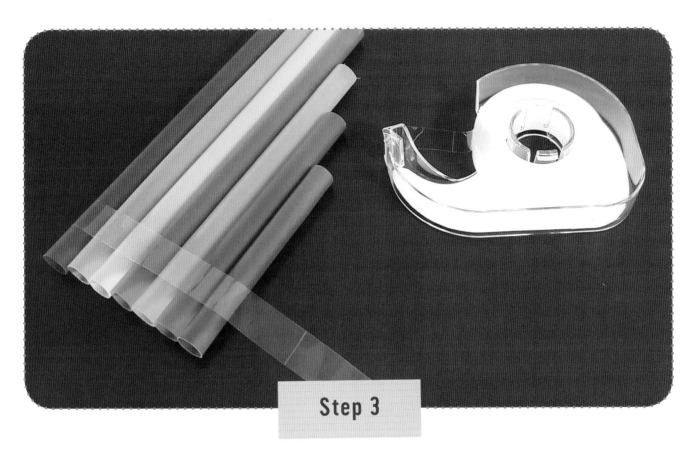

Step 3

Tape the straws on one side, then the other.

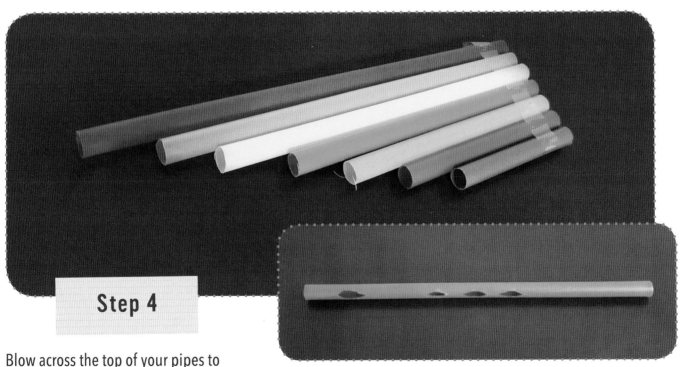

Step 4

Blow across the top of your pipes to make a light whistling noise. Do the longer or shorter straws produce the higher noise?

You can create a flute from a straw, too. Cut one hole to act as a mouth hole that you blow across. The other three holes act as finger holes. How does the pitch change when you cover one, two, or all three holes?

NOTES

BRAIN GAMES®

STEAM

ENGINEERING

HOW THINGS WORK

Publications International, Ltd.

Written by Nicole Sulgit and Beth Taylor
Photo styling by Nick LaShure and Nicole Sulgit
Photography by Christopher Hiltz, Nick LaShure and Nicole Sulgit
Additional images from Shutterstock.com

First printing
Manufactured in China.
03/2021 Guangdong

8 7 6 5 4 3 2 1

SAFETY WARNING
All of the experiments and activities in this book MUST be performed with adult supervision. All projects contain a degree of risk, so carefully read all instructions before you begin and make sure that you have safety materials such as goggles, gloves, etc. Also make sure that you have safety equipment, such as a fire extinguisher and first aid kit, on hand. You are assuming the risk of any injury by conducting these activities and experiments. Publications International, Ltd. will not be liable for any injury or property damage.

Let's get social!
⊙ @Publications_International
ⓕ @PublicationsInternational
ⓕ @BrainGames.TM
www.pilbooks.com

CONTENTS

INTRODUCTION

STEAM stands for science, technology, engineering, art, and math. In *How Things Work,* you'll be engineering as you build and test, but you'll also be exploring scientific principles, using math, and using and building different technologies. You might use your artistic side as well!

While we include step-by-step instructions for each experiment, you may find a different way to do things. If an experiment leaves you with questions, you can create your own experiments and try to answer them.

Engineers follow a certain set of steps as they work, called the Engineering Design Process. There are usually 5 to 7 steps that include identifying a problem that needs solving, researching it, brainstorming and planning a solution, testing that solution, and refining the plan based on the results. One simple 5-step Engineering Design Process uses these words: Ask, Imagine, Plan, Create, Improve.

ASK

What is the problem? What do you know about the problem? Have other people tried to solve the problem? What materials do you have available to solve the problem?

IMAGINE

How might you solve the problem? How many ideas can you come up with? As you work, you might find yourself asking more questions, too!

PLAN

Of your potential solutions, which seems best? What materials do you need? What do you expect the finished product to look like? Engineers often produce sketches or diagrams.

CREATE

Engineers don't move straight from a diagram to a finished product. Instead, they create a model called a prototype. They see how it works—or doesn't work!

IMPROVE

You can learn from problems as well as successes! From problems, you can learn how to improve the prototype. Sometimes, you'll go back to the drawing board and brainstorm a new solution.

MONITORING THE WORLD

Today, we have a lot of ways to monitor our world. We can check a weather forecast to see what kind of clothes to wear, glance at a smartphone to see the time, and use a GPS to tell us how to get from one place to another. In the past, scientific instruments were simpler.

Most car dashboards show time and temperature.

AIR PRESSURE

We can't see the air, but that does not mean it doesn't have weight. Layers of air higher in Earth's atmosphere put pressure on the air layers closer to the Earth. As these areas of high or low pressure change or move, they affect the weather. Tools called barometers measure air pressure, which helps people make weather forecasts.

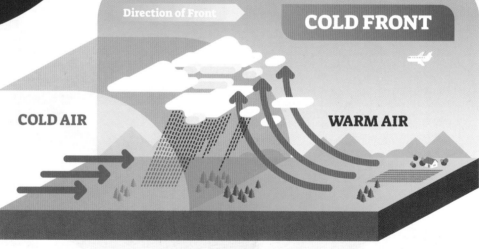

Direction of Front

COLD FRONT

COLD AIR

WARM AIR

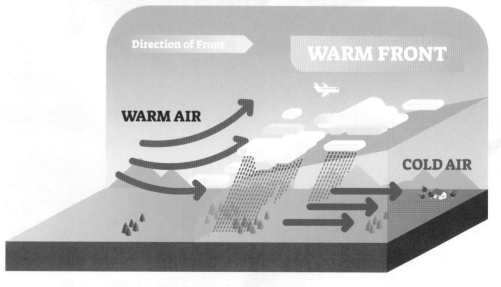

Direction of Front

WARM FRONT

WARM AIR

COLD AIR

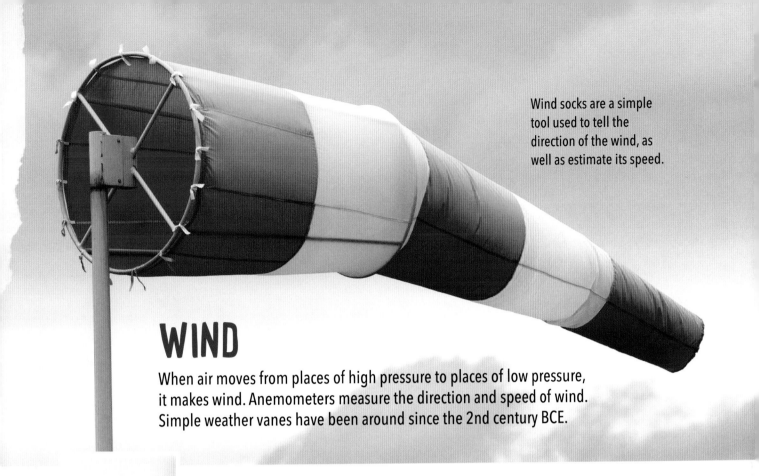

Wind socks are a simple tool used to tell the direction of the wind, as well as estimate its speed.

WIND

When air moves from places of high pressure to places of low pressure, it makes wind. Anemometers measure the direction and speed of wind. Simple weather vanes have been around since the 2nd century BCE.

TEMPERATURE

Where does the word Fahrenheit come from? Daniel Gabriel Fahrenheit (1686-1736) was a physicist and inventor who invented an accurate thermometer that used mercury. While thermometers had existed before that point, they weren't very reliable. In many other countries, and in scientific studies, people use the Celsius or centigrade scale to measure temperature. It is named after Anders Celsius (1701-1744), who was a Swedish astronomer and physicist.

HUMIDITY

If you're asked to think of water, you'll probably imagine its liquid form. But it's around in its solid form as ice, and it's present in the air in its gaseous form, water vapor. Hygrometers measure how humid the air is—that is, how much water vapor is in it.

WIND VANE

You can make a wind vane from simple materials you have at home.

MATERIALS

- 1 large plastic cup
- 4 small paper cups
- Gravel or small stones
- Glue
- Tape
- Scissors
- Straw
- Marker
- Ribbon spool
- Lightweight cardstock
- 4 craft sticks

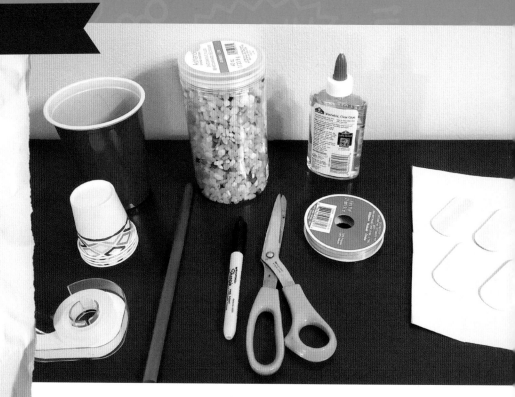

Step 1

Trace and cut out two cardboard circles the size of the top of the plastic cup.

8

Step 2

Fill the bottom of the plastic cup with gravel or small pebbles to weigh it down.

Step 3

Using the end of the scissors, poke a hole through the center of each cardboard circle. Each hole should easily allow the straw to pass through. Tape down one cardboard circle to the plastic cup with the straw in place.

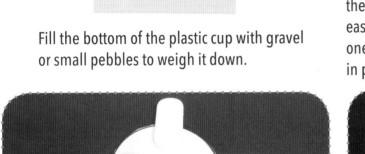

Step 4

Secure the craft sticks to the second cardboard circle with glue and/or tape.

Step 5

Secure the four paper cups to the craft sticks with glue and/or tape. Draw on one to distinguish it from the others.

Step 6

Put the ribbon spool on top of the plastic cup. It acts as a turntable that allows the top of your wind vane to move smoothly.

Step 7

Place the top of your wind vane on the bottom cup. Make sure it spins freely. How many times does the marked cup spin by in a minute?

HOT AIR

Did you know that air expands when it is heated? The molecules move faster and further apart. This simple experiment illustrates that point.

MATERIALS

- Empty soda bottle
- Balloon
- Container of hot water

Step 1

Stretch out the empty balloon. Secure it on the end of the empty bottle.

Step 2

Place the bottle into the container of hot water. The balloon expands!

HOW DOES IT WORK?

When air is heated, the molecules inside move faster. They also move further apart. Hot air is less dense than cold air. When the plastic soda bottle conveys the heat from outside, the air inside the bottle expands. It has no place to go except into the balloon. As the water cools, or if you take it out, the balloon will deflate again. Thermometers with a thin tube of liquid inside, such as mercury, work on the same principle. The liquid expands as it gets hotter, rising in the tube.

BAROMETER

You can't measure exact air pressure with this homemade barometer, but you can measure a change in air pressure.

MATERIALS

- Jar
- Balloon
- Rubber band
- Straw
- Tape
- Ruler
- Construction paper or other sturdy paper
- Scissors
- Pen

Step 1

Cut off the bottom from a balloon.

Step 2

Fit the top of the balloon over the top of the jar.

Step 3

Secure it with a rubber band.

Step 4

Tape a straw to the top of the jar.

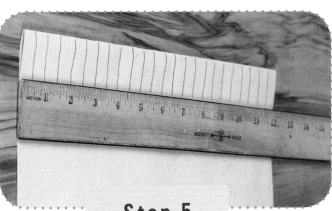

Step 5

Fold the paper in half. Draw lines at regular intervals on the sheet of paper.

Step 6

As the air pressure rises or falls, the straw will rise or fall as well. Place the jar in a place where the temperature will not change, as that will also affect the straw.

If you have a barometer, keep it next to your homemade barometer. Track changes in your own barometer and compare them to the actual one and the weather outside. How accurate is your barometer?

SUNDIAL

Before clocks, people marked the passage of time with sundials. Make your own!

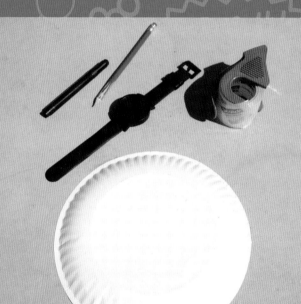

MATERIALS

- Paper plate
- Marker
- Pencil
- Tape
- Watch

Step 1

Carefully poke a hole in the center of the plate.

Step 2

Place the plate on the ground, with the pencil standing upright. In a sundial, the object that casts the shadow (here the pencil) is called the gnomen.

Tape the pencil in place.

Step 4

As the day passes, the pencil casts its shadow in different places. Mark where the shadow falls and the time.

Sculptors have to address practical issues when carrying out their creative vision. They need to make sure that things are balanced and strong, and that the sculpture has the support it needs.

STRONG SHAPES

Every new structure begins with a plan. Engines and machines are worked on by mechanical engineers. Civil engineers work on structures such as dams, bridges, and canals. Architects design houses and skyscrapers, working with a team of other specialists such as electrical and structural engineers. These professionals study shapes and materials. How can the structures they build best withstand forces such as wind, earthquakes, and time?

Today, most new houses in the United States have air conditioning. But air conditioning has only been around for about a century. Before that time, builders in areas that got hot in the summer had several strategies, such as shaded windows, for circulating air and staying cool.

Some civil engineers specialize in making sure buildings can stand against earthquakes.

Available materials often affect shapes and structures. When pioneers were settling the Great Plains, they did not always have wood to build houses. Instead, they used sod, a combination of grass and soil.

CRAFT STICK TRUSSES

Buildings and bridges are usually supported by a truss, a framework of beams or bars that are connected at their ends. An engineer's goal is to design a truss that won't bend or break. Find out what geometric shape forms the strongest truss in this experiment.

MATERIALS

7 jumbo craft sticks

7 small binder clips

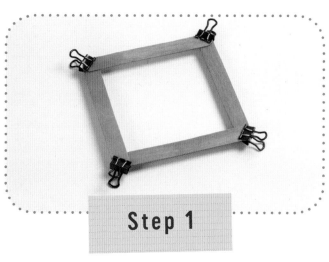

Step 1

Make a square with 4 craft sticks. Join the ends with a small binder clip at each corner.

Step 2

Grip 2 adjacent craft sticks and gently try to rotate them. *How easy is it to rotate the craft sticks?*

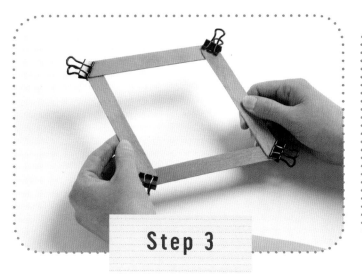

Step 3

Grip 2 craft sticks on opposite sides of the square and gently try to slide them back and forth parallel to each other. *How easy is it to slide the craft sticks? What happens to the shape of the square?*

Step 4

Now make a triangle with 3 craft sticks. Join the ends with small binder clips.

Step 5

Grip 2 adjacent craft sticks and gently try to rotate them just like you did with the square. Try sliding the craft sticks back and forth. *How does the triangle compare with the square? Which shape makes the stronger truss?*

IN REAL LIFE!

See how triangles work in a real life bridge!

HOW DOES IT WORK?

You probably found that it was easy to rotate and slide the sticks in your square truss. Your square might have even turned into a parallelogram. But you probably couldn't rotate or slide the sticks in your triangle truss. That's because a triangle is a rigid shape. Structures built with triangles are much stronger than those built with only squares.

CRAFT STICK BRIDGE

Build your own truss bridge!

MATERIALS

- Craft sticks
- Wood glue
- Paper towels or newspapers to protect surfaces from glue

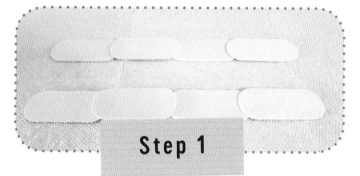

Step 1

Lay out the sides of the bottom of your bridge using 4 overlapping craft sticks on each side. Use dabs of glue to join them together.

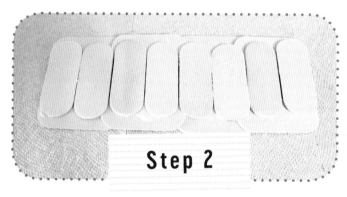

Step 2

Fill in the bottom of your bridge with craft sticks acting as planks. Set the bottom aside to dry completely.

Step 3

The sides of your bridge will be formed with triangles. Begin with one, then create another that overlaps the first.

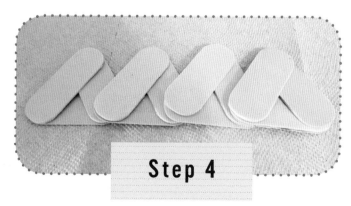

Step 4

The side should be as long as the bottom of the bridge.

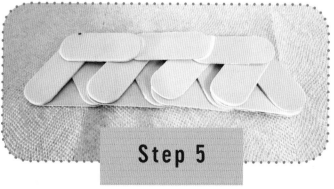

Step 5

Add craft sticks to form the top. Create a second side using the same steps. Set both pieces aside to dry completely.

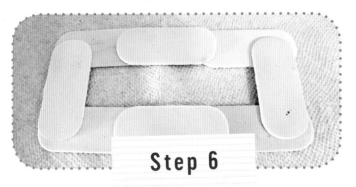

Step 6

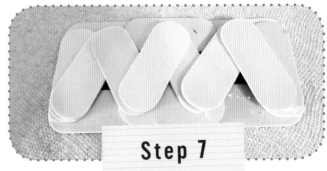

Step 7

Create a rectangle of craft sticks to form the top of the bridge.

Strengthen the top by filling it in with triangles. Set the piece aside to dry completely.

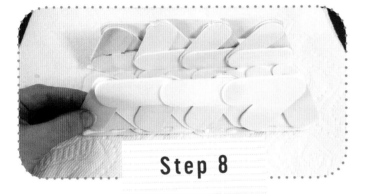

Step 8

When all sides of the bridge have dried, glue each side to the bottom. Prop the sides in place to dry completely.

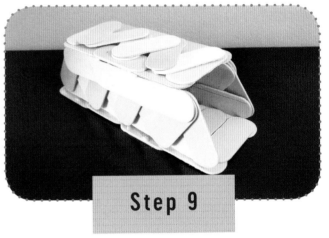

Step 9

Glue the top to the piece and let it dry completely overnight.

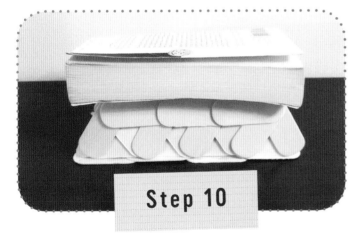

Step 10

Test your bridge. How much weight can it take?

Step 11

Use books and add them one by one.

Step 12

When the bridge cracks, weigh the books on a scale. See how much weight your bridge carried. Try different designs to see if that affects how much weight the bridge carries!

ENERGY

In science, energy is the ability to do work. Sometimes energy is stored to be used later. This is called potential energy. When an object is moving, it is using kinetic energy.

An arrow about to be released has potential energy. An arrow in motion has kinetic energy.

MANY KINDS OF ENERGY

There are many kinds of energy, including heat energy, light energy, chemical energy that comes from chemical reactions, and electrical energy. Some sources of energy are renewable. For example, we can keep harnessing solar energy from the Sun. Other sources of energy are not renewable. Think of a campfire. You use wood to generate light and heat. But once a piece of wood is burned, it cannot be used again.

THREE LAWS OF MOTION

Sometimes if we watch an object move–a ball bouncing downhill–it seems random. But objects in motion follow certain rules. In the 1600s, Sir Isaac Newton described three laws of motion.

FIRST LAW OF MOTION

The first law says that an object at rest remains at rest, while an object in motion stays in motion, with the same direction and speed. Let's say a ball is sitting on the ground. Unless someone exerts a force on it by kicking it or pushing it, or a wind exerts a force on it to move it, the ball will stay on the ground. It won't just spontaneously fly in midair. If you roll a ball along the ground, it will keep going in the direction you rolled it. If it does change direction, it will be because of an outside force, like a bump in the ground. When it slows down, it will be because of the outside force of gravity, and other forces like friction from the carpeting.

SECOND LAW OF MOTION

The second law of motion says that objects with a larger mass require more force to move them. There is an equation that says Force = mass times acceleration.

THIRD LAW OF MOTION

The third law of motion says that for every action, there is an equal and opposite reaction. When you push on a wall, you are exerting a force on it. But the wall is also exerting a force in the opposite direction!

FRICTION

One of the forces that acts on a moving object is friction. When you roll a ball, it will eventually come to a halt because of friction. Some materials cause more friction than others. A wet floor provides less friction than a dry one!

CRAFT STICK BOMBS

Weave craft sticks together to create stick bombs. Then find out what happens when kinetic energy is released.

TRIANGLE BOMB

Step 1

Arrange 3 craft sticks in an upside-down triangle as shown. Add small binder clips where the sticks meet.

Step 2

Place another stick on top of the upside-down triangle in the middle.

Step 3

Weave the final stick under one side of the triangle, over the middle stick, and then under the other side of the triangle.

Step 4

Carefully remove the small binder clips to complete the triangle bomb. Tension will hold the stick bomb together until it hits something and the kinetic energy is released.

Step 5

In an empty area, throw your triangle bomb on the floor or another surface and watch it explode!

SQUARE BOMB

Step 1

Arrange 2 craft sticks in a T shape as shown with the middle stick under the top stick. Add a small binder clip where the sticks meet.

Step 2

Place 2 sticks on the sides, parallel with the middle stick, and overlapping the top stick. Add small binder clips where sticks meet.

Step 3

In the middle of the square you are creating, weave a stick over a side stick, under the middle stick, and then over the other side stick.

Step 4

At the bottom of the square you are creating, weave a stick under a side stick, over the middle stick, and then under the other side stick.

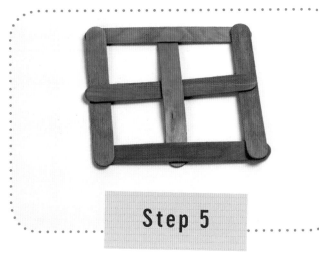

Step 5

Carefully remove the binder clips to complete the square bomb.

HOW DOES IT WORK?

Craft stick bombs are held together under tension. You create the tension by weaving the sticks together. These interwoven sticks can store a surprising amount of potential energy. When one key stick is dislodged, the energy is released, causing the entire stick bomb to explode into pieces.

EGGS-PERIMENT

An egg thrown directly at a wall will break. An egg thrown at a curved sheet stands a better chance. The sheet slows down the motion of the egg so that there is less of an impact. A car's airbags work on the same principles.

MATERIALS

- A sheet
- Two chairs
- Eggs
- Tape

Step 1

Attach a sheet on both sides to trees or posts. Do not tape it to a wall.

Step 2

Attach the bottom corners to two chairs. The sheet should form a slope.

Grab some eggs. (Make sure to wash your hands after handling raw eggs.)

Step 4

Throw them at the sheet!

They don't break! Why not? If you threw an egg straight at a wall, it would break. But the sheet slows down the egg's motion over a longer period of time.

RUBBER BAND SLINGSHOT

Turn potential energy into kinetic energy with a simple slingshot.

MATERIALS

- Two rubber bands
- Tape
- Paper or other soft material to propel with your slingshot

Safety note

Make sure you do not use hard material in your slingshot. Make sure anyone in the room is behind the slingshot when you use it.

Step 1

Put the two rubber bands so that they overlap slightly.

Step 2

Draw the rubber band on the right over the other rubber band, then underneath it and through the rubber band, to form a knot.

Step 3

Cut a length of tape to use as the cradle.

Step 4

Wrap the tape around the rubber band as a cradle.

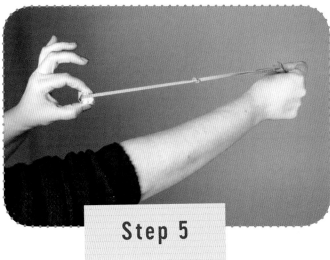

Step 5

Crumple up a ball of paper or a napkin and place it in the cradle. Pinch the paper in one hand while stretching the other end of the slingshot with your other hand.

Step 6

Release the slingshot! The paper ball goes flying.

EXPERIMENT MORE!

Experiment with the angle of your slingshot. What works best–for your hands to be level, or for one to be higher than the other? How does stretching the rubber band or using different sizes of rubber bands affect the experiment? How high can you shoot the paper ball? How far can you shoot it?

BALLOON ROCKET

Explore the physics behind thrust as you launch a balloon rocket.

- Balloon
- Plastic straw
- 10-foot length of string
- 2 chairs
- Scissors
- Tape
- Small binder clip
- Ruler or measuring tape

Step 1

Position chairs about 6–8 feet (1.8–2.4 m) apart with clear space in between. Tie one end of the string to one of the chairs.

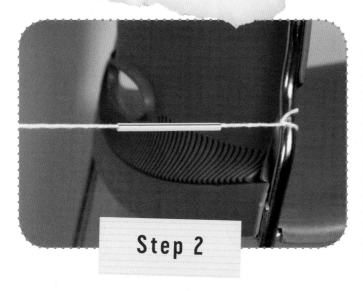

Step 2

Cut a piece of straw approximately 2 inches (5 cm) long. Run the free end of the string through the piece of straw.

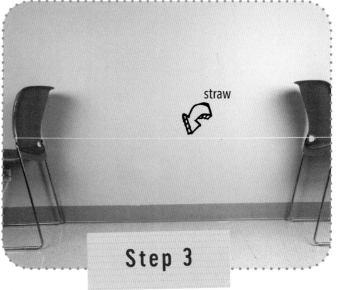

straw

Step 3

Pull the string going through the straw tight and tie the free end to the other chair.

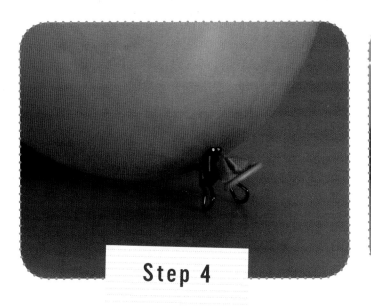

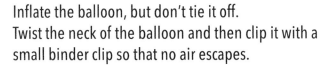

Step 4

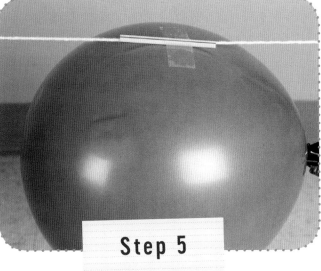

Step 5

Inflate the balloon, but don't tie it off.
Twist the neck of the balloon and then clip it with a small binder clip so that no air escapes.

Tape the balloon to the straw so that the closed neck faces towards one of the chairs.

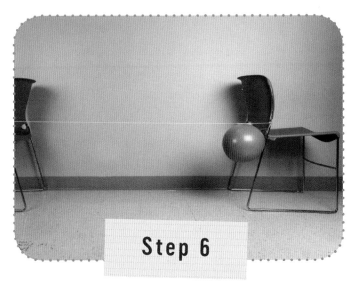

Step 6

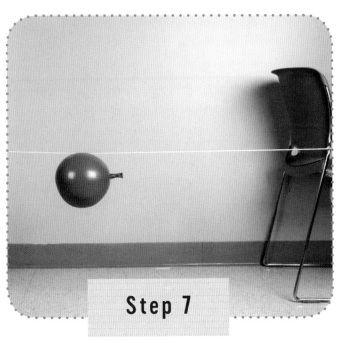

Step 7

Pull the balloon to one end of the string so that its closed neck is close to that chair. *What do you think will happen when you release the balloon?*

Release the balloon's closed neck and watch it speed down its launch path!

HOW DOES IT WORK?

Your balloon rocket works thanks to thrust. When you inflated the balloon, you pushed air into it. When you released the closed neck, the air rushing out of the balloon created forward motion called thrust. Thrust is the pushing force that moved your balloon rocket along its launch path. In a real rocket launch, thrust is created by the force of burning rocket fuel as it blasts from the rocket's engine. As the engines blast down, the rocket goes up.

CONFETTI CANNON

Make a fun party favor with just a balloon, tape, and a toilet paper tube!

- Toilet paper tube
- Balloon
- Scissors
- Masking tape or painter's tape
- Large pieces of confetti

Potential vs. Kinetic

This experiment is a great example of the transformation of potential energy (when you are holding the end of the balloon) to kinetic energy (when you release the balloon). The confetti is propelled into the air by that energy.

Step 1

Tie a knot at the end of the balloon.

Step 2

Cut off the top of the balloon. Cut off enough that the balloon will fit comfortably over the toilet paper tube.

Step 3

Fit the balloon over one end of the toilet paper tube.

Step 4

Tape the balloon to the tube with a strong tape such as masking tape.

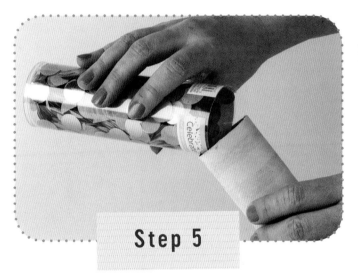

Step 5

Pour some confetti into the open end of the tube. Let it fall into the balloon. Don't use so much confetti that it clogs the tube.

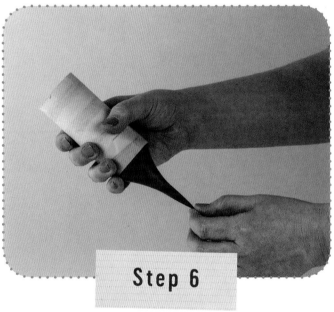

Step 6

Pull down the end of the balloon.

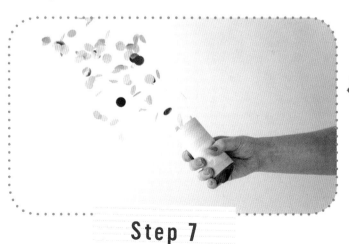

Step 7

Release the balloon. Confetti everywhere!

The party favor is re-usable—you can load it up with confetti and run the experiment again. Have fun and decorate it! Try a few different variations: use something heavier than confetti such as small fabric pompoms. Try more or less confetti—does the amount of confetti in the tube affect how far it goes? Does the amount you stretch the balloon in step 6 affect the amount of confetti released or how far it goes?

WINDMILL

Make your own windmill model to see how one works.

MATERIALS

- 1 large plastic cup
- 2 small plastic cups
- 2 toilet paper cardboard tubes
- Cardboard
- Glue
- Painter's tape
- String or thread
- Small object such as a paper clip or safety pin
- Chopstick or skewer
- Adhesive putty

Step 1

Poke holes in the bottom of each paper cup.

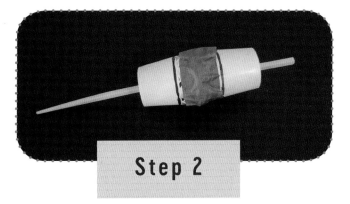

Step 2

Tape the cups together, facing each other. Poke the skewer through them.

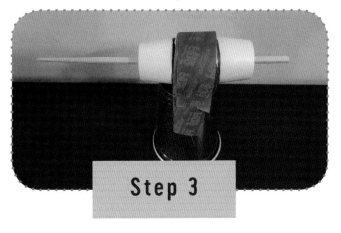

Step 3

Tape the cups to the larger plastic cup that will act as your windmill base.

People harness energy from the wind through windmills and wind turbines. Windmills have been around for centuries. In older days, the wind would turn the blades, which would set other parts of the windmill in motion in order to grind flour. Today, wind power can be transformed into electrical power.

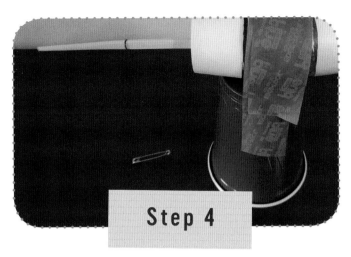

Step 4

Secure your paper clip or safety pin to one end of the skewer with string. It will be the load you are trying to lift.

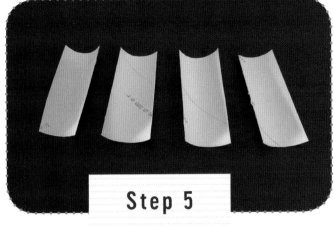

Step 5

Cut the toilet paper tubes to make four slightly curved blades.

Step 6

Cut two long strips from the cardboard and glue them to the blades.

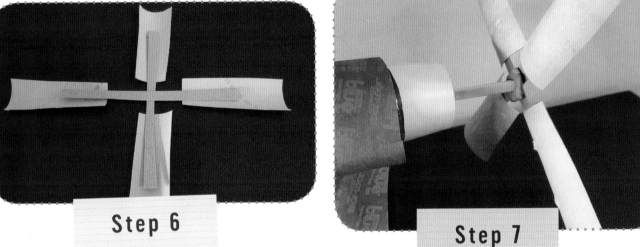

Step 7

Secure the blades to the end of the skewer with adhesive putty.

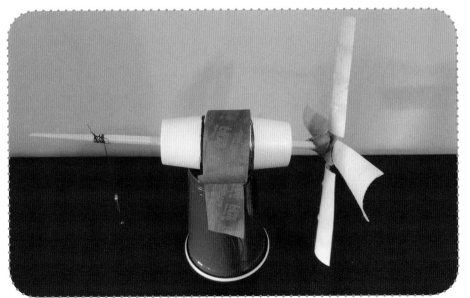

Step 8

Turn the blades. As you do, see how the skewer turns, lifting the safety pin off the ground.

SOLAR DISTILLER

Solar energy can be used to purify water. Wait for a hot, sunny day to perform this experiment.

MATERIALS

- 1 cup of water
- 1 tablespoon of salt
- Food coloring
- Large bowl
- Small bowl
- Plastic wrap
- Small stone

Step 1

Pour salt into the water to act as a contaminant.

Step 2

Mix the water and salt until it is cloudy.

Step 3

If desired, add some food coloring.

Step 4

Pour the mixture into the large bowl.

Step 5

Place the small bowl into the large bowl.

Step 6

Cover the bowls with plastic wrap.

Step 7

Place a stone or other small weight on the wrap.

Step 8

Leave the bowl in direct sunlight. You will begin to notice condensation gathering on the plastic wrap and dripping into the small bowl.

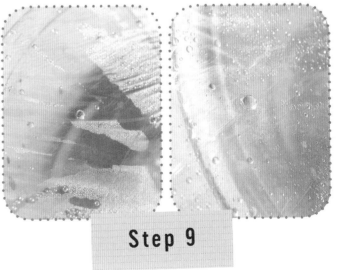

Step 9

Energy from the sun heats the water. It evaporates, and then condenses on the plastic wrap. When it drips into the small bowl, it is free of salt.

SOUND

Sound is a kind of energy that moves in waves. Sound waves are created when objects vibrate. Fast vibrations produce high sounds, while slower vibrations produce lower sounds.

HOW SOUND TRAVELS

Sound waves can travel through air, water, or other materials. Some materials are better conductors of sound than others. Metals conduct sound very well, while soft materials like paper tend to muffle sound. When engineers, architects, and decorators are designing a space, they need to pay attention to how sound will work in that space—they study its acoustics. A concert hall or an auditorium will be designed to best transmit the sounds from the stage. Restaurants, by contrast, may want to use materials such as acoustic ceiling tiles that absorb sound so that people can converse easily.

THE SPEED OF SOUND

Sound travels at different speeds depending on the material it is traveling through. In air, sound travels more than 750 miles per hour (343 meters/second). In water, it moves even faster: more than 3,310 miles per hour (1,480 meters/second).

SOUND IN SPACE?

Sound can travel through different states of matter—solid, liquid, or gas. But it can't travel if there is no matter. Since space is a vacuum, sound doesn't travel through space.

VOCAL CORDS

How do humans create sound? One way to create sound is to speak. When you speak, you are using two folds of muscle tissue in your throat called vocal cords. When you breathe, your vocal cords are open. When you speak, they vibrate to create sound.

ORIGAMI POPPER

Can paper make a noise louder than a quiet rustle? If you fold it the right way, it can.

Step 1

Fold the paper in half from top to bottom. Unfold it.

Step 2

Fold the paper in half from left to right. Unfold it.

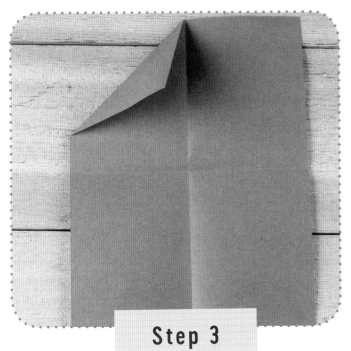

Step 3

Fold one corner in towards the center of the origami model.

Step 4

Fold the other three corners in the same way.

Step 5

Rotate the model.

Step 6

Bring the top of the paper down along the center fold.

Take the left corner. Fold it down at the center line. Do the same with the right corner.

Step 8

Flip the model over and rotate it as shown.

Step 9

Fold the model in half.

Step 10

If you hold it at one end, it should look like this.

Step 11

Hold the model by the points at the other end. Make sure you are not holding onto the interior folds.

Step 12

In a quick whipping motion, flick the model in the air. The interior folds will pop out, making a sound.

Step 13

If you don't get good results the first time, loosen the interior folds and try again.

LOUDSPEAKERS

Make loudspeakers for your smartphone with simple paper products.

MATERIALS

- Paper towels
- Paper towel roll
- Two paper cups
- Scissors
- Smartphone
- Pen

Step 1

Measure your phone against the paper towel roll and draw a slot where it will go.

Step 2

Cut a slot in the paper towel roll.

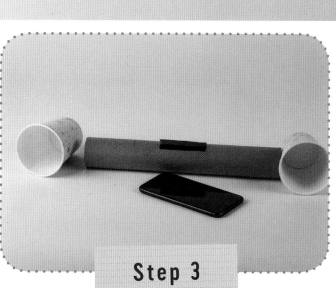

Step 3

The cups will go on either side of the paper towel roll.

Step 4

Draw a circle on each cup that matches the diameter of the paper towel roll.

Step 6

Crumple a paper towel into each end of the paper towel roll.

Step 8

Fit your phone in the slot and play a song! What do you notice about the music? If you remove the paper towels, how does that affect the song?

Step 5

Cut holes in the paper cups.

Step 7

Fit the cups to the paper towel roll.

FOR FURTHER TESTING

Try just putting your phone in a cup or bowl. Does that amplify or dampen the sound? Does it depend on the material? Try plastic, glass, and ceramic.

NOISY SPOONS

This simple experiment shows how well solid objects conduct sound.

MATERIALS

- Several metal spoons
- Yarn
- Scissors
- Tape

Step 1

Cut a length of yarn several feet long.

Step 2

Tape the spoons to the yarn. They should be close enough that the free ends of the spoons can clank together.

Step 3

The spoons clink and make noise.

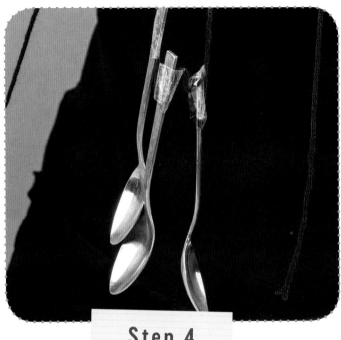

Step 4

Now hold the ends of the yarn up to your ears. Does it sound different? Do you think it sounds better or worse?

HOW DOES IT WORK?

The vibrations of the sound waves travel up the yarn to your ears. Because solid objects carry sound better than air, you will hear a difference in the quality of the sound.

FOR FURTHER FUN

Connect two paper cups to each other with a long length of string. Speak normally into the cup to a friend or sibling at the other end. How far apart can you get and still be heard?

ELECTRICITY

When you turn on a light at home, or use a laptop, you're using electricity. But what is electricity? How do people harness it?

Electricity sounds similar to "electrons"–the negative particles found in atoms. There's a reason for that. In a neutral state, an atom has the same number of protons and electrons. The electrons are on the outside of the atom, with the protons on the inside. When atoms gain or lose electrons, it creates a charged state. If you have a group of atoms and their electrons are made to move from one atom to another, it creates electricity.

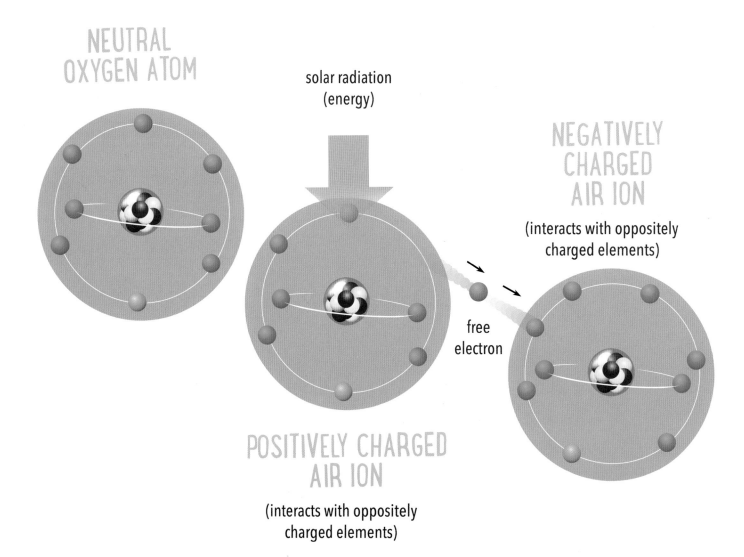

NEUTRAL
OXYGEN ATOM

solar radiation
(energy)

NEGATIVELY
CHARGED
AIR ION

(interacts with oppositely
charged elements)

free
electron

POSITIVELY CHARGED
AIR ION

(interacts with oppositely
charged elements)

CIRCUITS

An electric current moves through what is called a circuit. Let's say you turn on a light–when you click the switch, you are completing a circuit that allows the electric current to flow. Some materials such as metals are called conductors; they are very good at allowing electricity to flow through them. Other materials, called insulators, tend to slow down or halt an electric current.

LIGHTNING

Lightning is a form of electricity. Movement inside a thundercloud causes electrons to flow to the bottom of the cloud, while a positive charge of protons moves to the top. The negative charge tries to rejoin the positive charge by moving within a cloud, to another cloud, or to the ground. Lightning rods are made of conductive metal that can channel lightning safely to the ground.

Batteries store electric energy.

JUMPING LEAVES

Can you use the invisible forces of static electricity to make tissue paper leaves jump up without touching them?

Balloon

Tissue paper

Something wool

Pencil

Scissors

Step 1

Lay a single sheet of tissue paper flat on a table. Use a pencil to gently draw several leaves, each about 1½ inches (3.8 cm) long, onto the paper.

Step 2

Use scissors to carefully cut out the leaves. Place the cut-out leaves on a table.

Step 3

Inflate the balloon to its full size and tie off. Move the balloon a couple inches above the leaves. *Do you notice how nothing happens with the leaves?*

Step 4

Rub the balloon against something wool, such as a scarf or blanket, for about one minute. If you don't have anything wool, rub the balloon on your hair. The balloon is now electrically charged.

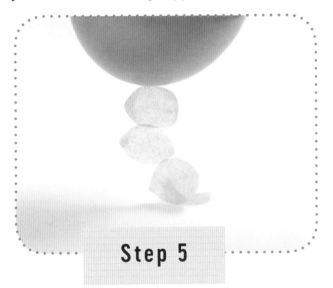

Step 5

Bring the charged balloon a few inches above the leaves and slowly move it closer. *What happens?* The leaves will be attracted to the balloon and eventually jump up toward it.

NOW TRY THIS!

Rub the balloon on wool as before. Bring the charged balloon close to a thin stream of running water. Watch the water bend toward the balloon.

HOW DOES IT WORK?

Static electricity is the buildup of electric charge in an object. Tiny particles called protons and electrons carry electric charge. Protons carry a positive (+) charge, and electrons carry a negative (-) charge. Objects that have opposite charges will attract, or pull together. Objects with the same charge will repel, or push apart. When you rub the balloon on wool, it picks up extra electrons, giving the balloon a negative charge. This pushes the electrons away in the paper, leaving a positive charge on the paper leaves. The negatively-charged balloon attracts the positively-charged paper leaves, causing them to jump up.

LEMON BATTERY

Make a battery using lemons. Then find out if your lemon battery can make an electric current flow around a circuit with enough energy to illuminate a small lamp called a light emitting diode (LED).

- 5 copper nails
- 5 zinc nails
- LEDs
- 6 short electrical wires with clips at each end
- 5 lemons
- Sharp knife

Step 1

Begin by rolling the lemons on a table to get them softer and juicier. With an adult's help, use a sharp knife to cut two slits in each lemon. The slits should be about 1¼ inches (3 cm) apart and about ½ inch (1¼ cm) deep.

Step 2

For each lemon, insert a galvanized (zinc-covered) nail into one slit and a copper nail into the other. Arrange the lemons in a circle with the zinc nails next to the copper nails in the adjacent lemons.

Step 3

Squeeze open the clip on one side of an electrical wire and fasten it onto a copper nail. Fasten the clip on the other side onto a zinc nail in the next lemon.

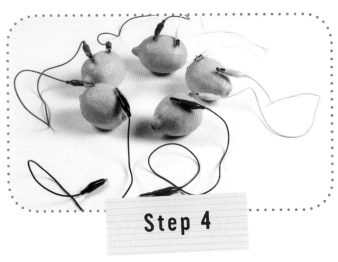

Step 4

Connect all of the lemons—copper nail to zinc nail—as in step 3, except for the first and last lemons. Instead, fasten a clip onto the first lemon's zinc nail and leave the other clip unconnected. Fasten a clip onto the last lemon's copper nail and leave the other clip unconnected.

Step 5

Each LED has two legs that are slightly different lengths. With the free end of the wire that is attached to the copper nail, fasten the clip onto the slightly longer leg of the LED.

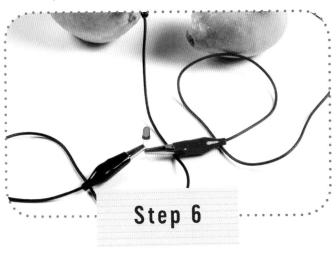

Step 6

With the free end of the wire attached to the zinc nail, fasten the clip onto the shorter leg of the LED. This completes the circuit to make the LED light up. The LED is very faint, so you might want to dim other lights to see it.

HOW DOES IT WORK?

The electric current that lights your LED is actually caused by countless tiny particles called electrons moving around the circuit. Electrons are present inside every atom. As the zinc dissolves in the lemon juice, two electrons are released from each atom of zinc (from the zinc-covered nail). All electrons are negatively charged, and they push apart as they move inside the wire. When they reach the copper nail, they take part in another chemical reaction, allowing electrons to continue flowing around the circuit.

MAGNETS

Your refrigerator at home may be full of them, holding up to-do lists or artwork or just adding a splash of decorative fun. Have you ever wondered why magnets stick on a refrigerator door but not, say, on a wooden door?

OPPOSITES ATTRACT

Certain objects generate a magnetic field. In a magnetic field, all the electrons spin in the same direction. The Earth itself is a giant magnet that generates a magnetic field. Just like the Earth has a North and South Pole, where its magnetic fields are strongest, so do smaller magnets. Each small magnet has a "north" and "south" pole. If you touch two magnets to each other, they will attract each other when the north pole of one magnet comes near the south pole of the other. But if you touch the north pole of one magnet against the north pole of another, the two magnets will repel each other.

MAGNETIC MATERIALS

A mineral called magnetite-it's also called lodestone–is a natural magnet. People would use lodestone in compasses that pointed to the North Pole of the Earth. Iron and some other metals like nickel are ferromagnetic–they're strongly attracted to magnets, and can hold a magnetic field. While magnets do affect other materials such as paper or wood, the effect is so weak that it isn't noticeable.

MAKING A MAGNET

Iron and steel can be made into a magnet pretty easily. You can make a metal paper clip into a temporary magnet, for example, by rubbing a magnet against the paperclip many times, making sure to always rub in the same direction. Electromagnets are created when people run an electric field through a metal, creating a permanent magnet.

MAGNETS IN USE TODAY

Magnets are used in electric motors, to store data in computers, and in medical scanners. The strip of material on the back of a credit card is a magnetic strip that stores data codes.

FLY A KITE

You don't need a windy day to fly this construction-paper kite.

MATERIALS

- Construction paper
- Scissors
- Tape (or glue)
- Yarn or string
- Metal paper clip
- Magnet*

*Magnets are available at craft stores and hardware stores

Step 1

Cut out kite pieces from the construction paper.

Step 2

Cut a piece of yarn the length of the kite.

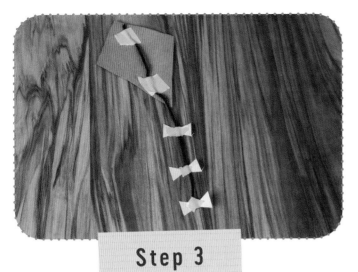

Step 3

Tape the yarn to the kite pieces. You can also use a dab of glue instead.

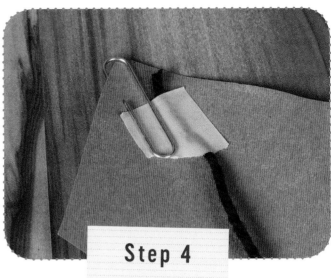

Step 4

Attach a metal paper clip to the top of the kite.

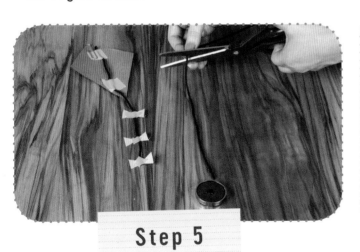

Step 5

For a circular magnet, thread your yarn through the hole in the magnet. For a bar magnet, use tape to attach the yarn to the magnet.

Step 6

When the magnet approaches the metal paper clip, it will lift the kite.

Step 7

Fly your kite!

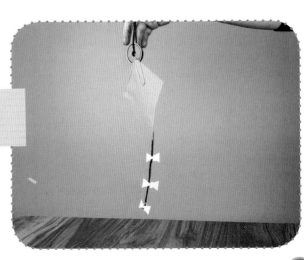

COMPASS

Which way is North? With this homemade compass, you'll always know the way.

MATERIALS

- Bowl
- Water
- Magnet*
- Needle (Metal)
- Cork*
- Scissors
- Tape
- Marker or pen

*You can often purchase magnets and cork at craft stores. Magnets are also found at hardware stores.

Step 1

Cut out a small piece of cork.

Step 2

Swipe the needle against the magnet at least 30 times, always in the same direction.

Step 3

Move the magnet away from your workspace. Tape the needle to the cork.

Step 4

Fill a bowl with water. Place your cork and needle in the bowl.

Step 5

The needle will point in a particular direction. You can verify by checking against a compass app on your smartphone that one end of the needle always points North.

Step 6

Mark "N" for North with a marker.

HOW DOES IT WORK?

In step 2, you are making the needle into a weak magnet. When it is close to the existing magnet, it will be attracted to it. But when the other magnet is moved away, the newly-magnetized needle then aligns itself with Earth's magnetic field.

SAFETY PIN CHAIN

Make paper clips or safety pins into weak magnets. How long can your chain get?

MATERIALS

- Safety pins or paper clips
- Two magnets

Step 1

Put up one magnet on the refrigerator. Magnetize a safety pin by swiping it against the other magnet 20 or 30 times, in the same direction. Then attach it to the magnet on the fridge.

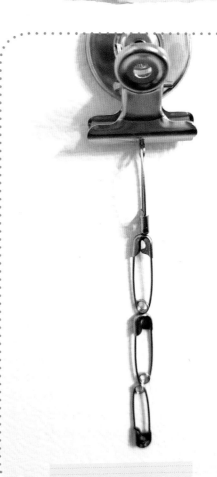

Step 2

Magnetize more safety pins. Attach them carefully, one by one. How long can your chain get before gravity wins out?

Step 3

You can also try to see how many safety pins you can attach to a single magnetized safety pin.

Step 4

What is your record? Can you start a second layer of safety pins?

NOTES

BRAIN GAMES®

STEAM

SCIENCE

KITCHEN CHEMISTRY

pil

Publications International, Ltd.

Written by Nicole Sulgit and Beth Taylor
Photo styling by Nick LaShure and Nicole Sulgit
Photography by Christopher Hiltz, Nick LaShure and Nicole Sulgit
Additional images from Shutterstock.com

Louis Weber, CEO
Publications International, Ltd.
8140 Lehigh Avenue
Morton Grove, IL 60053

First printing
Manufactured in China.
03/2021 Guangdong

8 7 6 5 4 3 2 1

SAFETY WARNING

All of the experiments and activities in this book MUST be performed with adult supervision. All projects contain a degree of risk, so carefully read all instructions before you begin and make sure that you have safety materials such as goggles, gloves, etc. Also make sure that you have safety equipment, such as a fire extinguisher and first aid kit, on hand. You are assuming the risk of any injury by conducting these activities and experiments. Publications International, Ltd. will not be liable for any injury or property damage.

Let's get social!
@Publications_International
@PublicationsInternational
@BrainGames.TM
www.pilbooks.com

CONTENTS

10

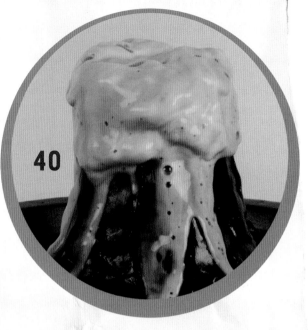

40

32

What do a rock, a river, and a raccoon have in common?

They are all made up of matter. Chemistry is the science that studies matter. What are substances made of? What are their properties? How do they interact with each other? How do they change?

ATOMS

One of the smallest building blocks of the universe is called the atom. Atoms are made up of positive particles called protons, negative particles called electrons, and neutral particles called neutrons. When an atom has the same number of protons and electrons, it is neutral. But atoms can gain or lose electrons. They are called ions when this happens.

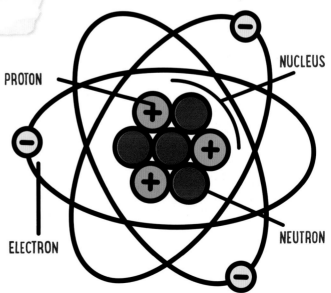

PROTON

NUCLEUS

ELECTRON

NEUTRON

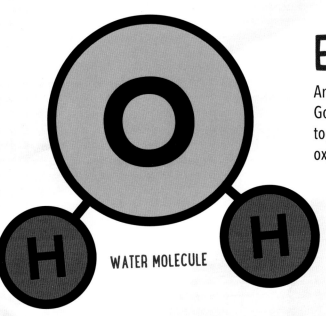

WATER MOLECULE

ELEMENTS

An element is a substance made up of a single type of atom. Gold, oxygen, and helium are all elements. Elements join together to form compounds. Water contains the elements of oxygen and hydrogen, for example.

HOW MANY ATOMS MAKE UP THE HUMAN BODY?

Billions and billions. In fact, **7,000,000,000,000,000,000,000,000,000**. The human body is mostly made up of the elements oxygen, carbon, hydrogen, nitrogen, calcium, and phosphorous. There are some other elements too, like sodium.

MASS

Mass is how much matter an object contains. Sometimes, a big object can have very little mass. A big sheet of paper could have less mass than a small rock. Mass is not exactly the same as weight. Weight is the force applied to the object by gravity. Your mass stays the same wherever you are in the universe, but your weight changes in places with more or less gravity. Someone who weighs 75 pounds on Earth would weigh about 175 pounds on Jupiter, but only about 5 pounds on Pluto!

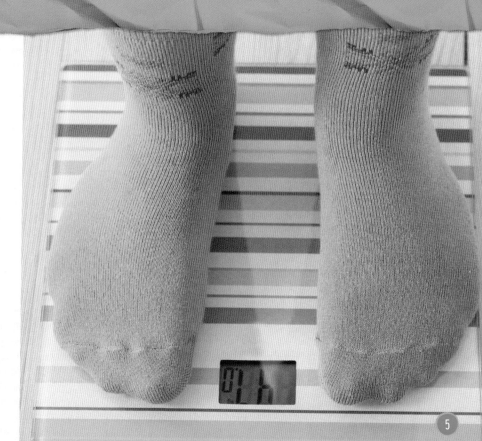

STATES OF MATTER

The same matter can exist in different states. For example, the compound H_2O, two hydrogen atoms combined with one oxygen atom, can exist as a solid in the form of ice, a liquid in the form of water, and a gas in the form of water vapor.

SOLID   LIQUID   GAS

In a solid state, molecules are tightly packed together. In a gas, they float more freely.

COLD   HOT

FROM STATE TO STATE

Temperature affects state. Each substance has a melting point where a solid becomes liquid and a freezing point where a liquid becomes solid. Many metals have a very high melting point. The melting point of gold, for example, is very high. That's why a gold necklace doesn't just melt in a puddle when it sits in a jewelry box. It needs to reach 1,948 degrees Fahrenheit or 1,064 degrees Celsius. Other metals, like Caesium, melt just above room temperature.

When a substance changes from gas to liquid, the process is called condensation. When a substance changes from liquid to gas, it is called vaporization.

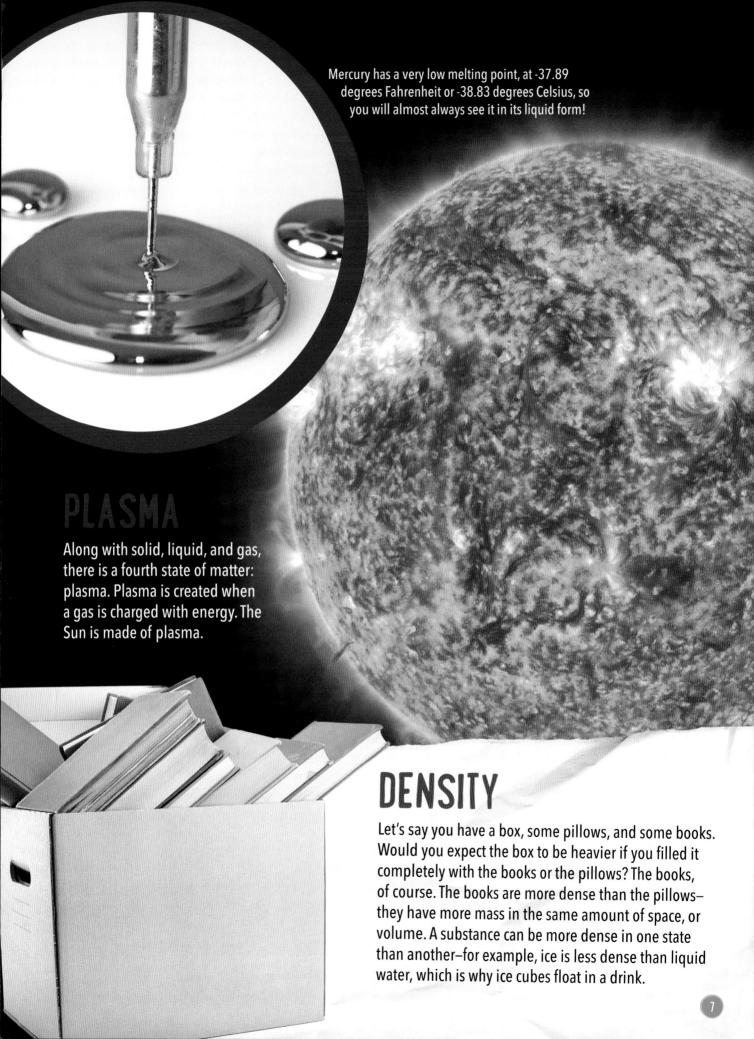

Mercury has a very low melting point, at -37.89 degrees Fahrenheit or -38.83 degrees Celsius, so you will almost always see it in its liquid form!

PLASMA

Along with solid, liquid, and gas, there is a fourth state of matter: plasma. Plasma is created when a gas is charged with energy. The Sun is made of plasma.

DENSITY

Let's say you have a box, some pillows, and some books. Would you expect the box to be heavier if you filled it completely with the books or the pillows? The books, of course. The books are more dense than the pillows—they have more mass in the same amount of space, or volume. A substance can be more dense in one state than another—for example, ice is less dense than liquid water, which is why ice cubes float in a drink.

SLIME

Make your own slime
and see how it behaves
differently from other liquids.

MATERIALS

- 1½–2 cups cornstarch
- 1 cup warm water
- ¼ cup shampoo
- Food coloring
- Wax paper
- Large mixing bowl
- Spatula
- Tablespoon

Step 1

Place wax paper on your work surface. Add 1½ cups
of cornstarch to the mixing bowl. Dip your hands in
the cornstarch. *What does the powder feel like?*

Step 2

Add ¼ cup shampoo to mixing bowl.

Step 3

Step 4

Mix a few drops of food coloring into a cup of warm water. Stir well with a tablespoon.

Add a few tablespoonfuls of colored water to the mixing bowl at a time. Keep stirring the water into the cornstarch with a spatula.

Step 5

Step 6

Continue adding water a few tablespoonfuls at a time until the mixture turns into a thick paste. Add cornstarch if the mixture gets too runny; add water if it becomes too thick.

Grab a handful of the slime and observe how it changes when you handle it different ways. *What happens when you roll it between your hands, squeeze it in your fist, press it onto a surface, or let it run through your fingers?*

HOW DOES IT WORK?

Slime isn't your typical liquid or solid. Applying pressure to the slime increases its viscosity, or thickness. When you handle the slime gently, the starch molecules can move around, suspended in the water. This makes a slow-flowing liquid.

But when you press down suddenly on the slime, the starch molecules lock together, making the slime feel more solid. Slime is an example of a non-Newtonian fluid. The viscosity of non-Newtonian fluids changes depending on the forces of pressure applied.

With pressure applied, slime feels more solid.

LIQUID LAYERS

Different liquids have different densities. Build a colorful tower by layering these liquids on top of each other.

MATERIALS

- Honey or maple syrup
- Water
- Vegetable or olive oil
- A measuring cup with a pouring spout
- A glass
- A variety of solid objects with different masses such as:
  - Berries
  - Grapes or cherry tomatoes
  - Coins
  - Marshmallows
  - Raisins or beans
- Food coloring (optional)

Step 1

Spoon or pour the honey or syrup into the bottom of a glass.

Step 2

If desired, add a few drops of food coloring to water. Slowly pour the water into the glass. You may want to tilt the glass at an angle for the best results.

Step 3

Because water is less dense than honey, it will settle on top of the honey.

Step 4

Pour the oil on top of the water. A slow, careful pour will work best.

Step 5

Begin gently dropping objects into the glass. *Do they settle to the bottom? Rest in the middle layer? Float on top?*

Coins settle to the bottom.

A bean is not quite as dense—it rests on top of the honey.

Blackberries are less dense than beans.

A marshmallow is very light!

ZOOMING BEANS

Defy gravity to make a bean "dance" in water!

MATERIALS

- Two glasses
- Bottled or tap water
- Carbonated water or clear carbonated soda
- Pinto beans

Step 1

Pour regular water into one glass, and a carbonated beverage into the other.

Step 2

Drop a few beans into each glass of water. *What happens?*

HOW DOES IT WORK?

The beans go up and down in the carbonated water. The bubbles of carbonation attach to the surface of the bean and lift it up. As bubbles pop and new bubbles reform, the bean falls and rises.

This experiment works best with fresh soda with many bubbles. Raisins are a great alternative if you don't have beans.

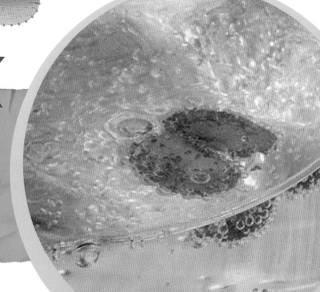

THE GROWING MARSHMALLOW

Create a marshmallow monster in your microwave!

MATERIALS

- Marshmallows
- Food coloring
- Toothpicks
- Microwave-safe plate
- Microwave

Step 1

Use toothpicks to dab food coloring on your marshmallows to decorate them.

Step 2

When done, put them on a plate that is safe to use in the microwave.

Marshmallows seem solid, but they have lots of air bubbles in them, along with sugar and water. When they heat up so quickly, the air bubbles expand, pushing against the stretchy walls of the molecule. The marshmallow expands.

Step 3

Microwave them for 1 minute. Watch them grow through the window! Watch them deflate as you pull them out of the microwave.

MINERALS AND CRYSTALS

Geologists study the materials that make up our Earth—rocks and minerals. You probably recognize the names of some of the most valuable minerals that can be made into gemstones. Amber, emerald, topaz, and diamond are all minerals. But there are thousands of minerals, some very obscure. Some are hard, while others are soft. Some are clear, while others are colorful. What do they have in common? They are all solid. They all occur in nature. They are not organic—that is, they are not made from living things. And each mineral has a fixed chemical makeup made up from the same combination of elements.

CRYSTALS

Many minerals have a crystalline structure. When you look at them through a microscope, their atoms or molecules are arranged in an orderly, repeating pattern.

The salt you use at the table is a mineral with a crystalline structure.

What does your pencil have in common with a diamond?

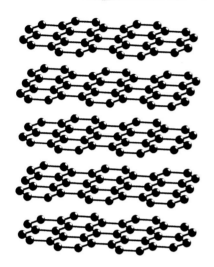

Both graphite and diamond are minerals made of a single element, carbon. But they have different crystalline structures.

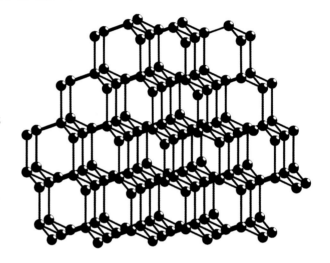

GRAPHITE

DIAMOND

TYPES OF MINERALS

Emerald and aquamarine are color variations of a silicate called beryl.

Scientists divide minerals into groups based on their chemical makeups. Silicates like quartz and feldspar are the most common minerals, and make up most of the Earth's top layer, its crust. All silicates contain the elements oxygen and silicon.

Some other important groups of minerals include carbonates and oxides. Carbonates contain carbon and oxygen. Oxides contain oxygen and a metal.

SALT AND PEPPER

Salt is a mineral, while pepper comes from a plant.
Use this trick to separate them if they get mixed up.

MATERIALS

- Salt
- Pepper
- Balloon

Step 1

Pour a small pile of salt and a small pile of pepper onto a flat surface.

Step 2

Mix the salt and pepper together.

Step 3

Inflate a balloon and rub it against a sweater to generate static electricity. Hold the balloon above your pile. Slowly lower it closer to the pile until the pepper begins to react.

Step 4

The pepper jumps up to the surface of the balloon! If you hold your balloon even closer, the salt will begin to jump up as well.

HOW DOES IT WORK?

Static electricity is the buildup of electric charge in an object. Protons carry a positive (+) charge, and electrons carry a negative (-) charge. Objects that have opposite charges will attract, or pull together. Objects with the same charge will repel, or push apart. When you rub the balloon on a sweater, it picks up extra electrons, giving the balloon a negative charge. This pushes the electrons away in the pile of salt and pepper, leaving a positive charge. The negatively-charged balloon attracts the positively-charged salt and pepper, causing them both to jump up. But since pepper is lighter, it jumps up more quickly.

If you don't have a balloon, you can charge a plastic fork or comb with static electricity in the same way and use that.

GROW A STALACTITE

In caves, stalactites form over years from mineral deposits. You can see the principles in action with this simple kitchen experiment.

MATERIALS

- Two jars or glasses
- A piece of yarn (about 1 foot long)
- Baking soda
- Water
- Paper clips
- Spoon
- Bowl
- Cardboard (optional)

Step 1

Spoon or pour baking soda into a jar of warm water. Stir until the water is cloudy and the baking soda begins to settle at the bottom of the jar instead of dissolving. Do the same with the other jar.

Step 2

Set up the jars with a bowl between them. It's best to do this on a surface that can be thrown out or easily wiped down, such as a piece of newspaper or cardboard. Because this experiment can take several days, it should also be somewhere out of the way.

Step 3

Step 4

Dip the ends of the yarn in each jar, so that they are resting in the water.

Secure the yarn to the jars with paper clips.

Step 5

Watch your stalactite grow over the next few days!

FOR FURTHER FUN

Try this experiment with sugar or salt, which also form crystals.

19

CHEMICAL REACTIONS

In a chemical reaction, one set of substances is changed into another set of substances. The first set of substances, the **reactants**, are transformed into **products** when the bonds between atoms in the reactants are broken so that new molecules can be formed.

Rust is the result of a chemical reaction. Iron and oxygen are the reactants. They transform into the product iron oxide.

Fire is a chemical reaction.

FAST OR SLOW

Some chemical reactions happen very quickly. Others happen more slowly. You can speed up a chemical reaction by increasing energy. Energy in the form of heat, for example, can speed up the chemical reactions that occur when you are baking something. Sometimes another substance, called a **catalyst,** can be added to the chemical reaction to speed it up. An **inhibitor** slows a chemical reaction down.

Kimchi, yogurt, and many pickles are all created through a chemical process called fermentation. Yogurt, for example, is created when bacteria are added to milk. The bacteria changes lactose, a sugar in the milk, into lactic acid.

THE AMAZING DISAPPEARING EGGSHELL

What chemical reaction occurs when an egg is immersed in vinegar? Try it and see.

MATERIALS

- Mason jars or glasses
- Egg(s)
- Vinegar
- Food coloring (optional)

Step 1

Fill a jar or jars with vinegar.

Step 2

For a cool effect, add food coloring.

Step 3

Add an egg to each jar or glass you use. Always wash your hands after handling raw eggs.

Step 4

Step 5

Put the eggs in the refrigerator. After several hours, you will see them begin to float to the top of the jar. You will see bubbles begin to form as well.

Leave the eggs in the refrigerator overnight.

What will you see when you draw them out?
THE EGGSHELL HAS DISAPPEARED!
Compared to a regular egg, the egg will also seem slightly larger.

WHERE DOES THE EGGSHELL GO?

Eggshell has a substance called calcium carbonate in it. The acid in vinegar breaks down the calcium carbonate. The bubbles are caused by the creation of carbon dioxide as it does so.

COLORFUL VEGGIES

Why do vegetables change colors as they are roasted?
Find out while you help prepare and eat dinner!

INGREDIENTS

- Vegetables
- Olive oil
- Seasonings such as salt, pepper, garlic powder

Step 1

Wash the vegetables. An adult should chop them up.

Step 2

Step 3

Add olive oil to coat the vegetables. Add seasoning.

Put the vegetables in a pan covered with foil.

Step 4

Step 5

Have an adult put them in an oven preheated to 425 degrees. As they cook, they begin to brown.

After fifteen or twenty minutes, your veggies will be ready to eat!

WHY DO VEGGIES BROWN AS THEY BAKE?

Heat changes vegetables, both their color and their taste. A chemical reaction called caramelization occurs that affects the natural sugars in the vegetables, deepening their color to brown and altering their flavor.

PANCAKE CHEMISTRY

With an adult, make pancakes and see chemical reactions happen.

INGREDIENTS

- 1 ½ cups flour
- 3 ½ teaspons baking powder
- 1 egg
- 3 tablespoons melted butter
- 1 ¼ cups milk
- 1 tablespoon white sugar

Step 1

Mix all the ingredients in a measuring cup or bowl.

Step 2

Do you see bubbles form? That is a chemical reaction caused by the baking powder.

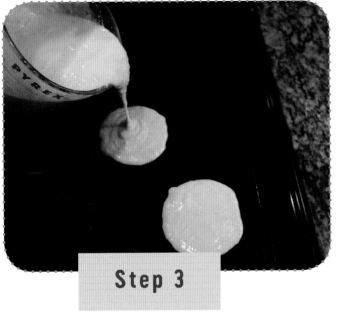

Step 3

An adult should pour the batter onto the griddle.

Step 4

Notice how bubbles form in the batter.

Step 5

An adult should flip the pancake over.

Step 6

Eat with syrup. *Why did the pancake turn brown?*

THE MAILLARD REACTION

When pancakes cook, they go through something called the Maillard reaction. Your ingredients contain both proteins, which have amino acids, and sugars. When heat is applied, the amino acids and the sugars go through a chemical reaction that produces the smell, the flavor, and the color of finished pancakes! The bubbles throughout the process are caused by the baking powder. It releases carbon dioxide.

SODA FOUNTAIN

Create a soda geyser with a chemical reaction between Mentos and Diet Coke.

MATERIALS

- Paper
- Tape
- Mentos
- 2 liter bottle of Diet Coke

Perform this experiment outdoors, using goggles or glasses. Keep your face away from the bottle.

Step 1

If you'd like, decorate the piece of paper.

Step 2

Roll the paper into a baton and tape it.

Step 3

Unscrew the lid of the soda bottle.

Step 4

Add a tube of Mentos to the tube of paper.

Step 5

Position the tube above the soda, keeping your finger on the end until you're ready to let them fall.

Step 6

Release the Mentos and step back!

ACIDS AND BASES

One way to classify a liquid is to ask whether it is an acid or a base. When you dissolve an acid in water, it releases a hydrogen ion–a positively charged hydrogen atom (H+). When you dissolve a base in water, it releases a hydroxide ion–a negatively charged molecule made from oxygen and hydrogen (OH-).

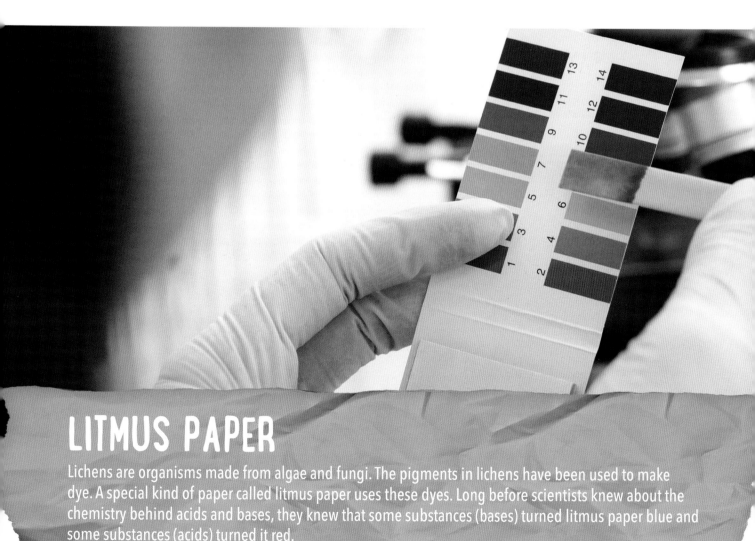

LITMUS PAPER

Lichens are organisms made from algae and fungi. The pigments in lichens have been used to make dye. A special kind of paper called litmus paper uses these dyes. Long before scientists knew about the chemistry behind acids and bases, they knew that some substances (bases) turned litmus paper blue and some substances (acids) turned it red.

pH SCALE

The 14-point pH scale is used to measure how basic or acidic a substance is when compared to water, which is neutral on the scale. Substances on either end of the scale that are strongly acidic or strongly basic (or alkaline) are dangerous to humans.

Have you ever had an upset stomach? Medicines like antacids work by neutralizing stomach acid.

Many acids taste sour to us. Citric acid gives grapefruit a sour flavor.

ACIDIC

0	battery	
1	stomach acid	
2	lemon	
3	soda	
4	tomato	
5	coffee	
6	milk	

NEUTRAL

7	water	
8	blood	
9	egg white	
10	stomach tablets	
11	ammonia solution	
12	soap	
13	bleach	
14	drain cleaner	

ALKALINE

PICKLES

Use the acid vinegar to transform cucumbers into pickles!

An adult should do all the cutting in this experiment.

- 3–4 pickling cucumbers
- 1 ½ teaspoons coarse-grained kosher salt
- ¼ cup white distilled vinegar

- 1 clove garlic (optional)
- ¼ teaspoon dill seed (optional)
- ¼ teaspoon mustard seed (optional)

Step 1

Have an adult cut the cucumbers into thin slices and add them to a one-pint Mason jar.

Step 2

Add the vinegar to the jar.

Step 3

Add 1 ½ teaspoons salt to the jar.

Step 4

Add ¼ teaspoon dill seeds.

Step 5

Add ¼ teaspoon mustard seeds.

Step 6

Have an adult mince the garlic and add it to the jar. Seal the jar. Note how high the vinegar rises and how high the cucumbers are in the jar. Shake the jar to mix the ingredients.

Step 7

Put the jar in the fridge. Shake it at the one hour mark.

Step 8

Check again and shake the jar at the two hour mark. Note that the height of the liquid in the jar has gone up, as the salt pulls the water out of the cucumbers. Taste test a pickle.

Step 9

Over the next several days, see how the taste of the pickles changes. They will also change color over time. In this picture, you can see a cucumber before it is put in the brine, a pickle at one day, and a pickle at one week.

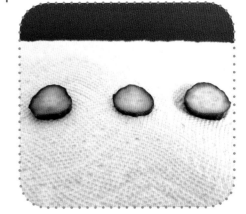

Fridge pickles last about two to three weeks. The salt and the vinegar are the key ingredients for changing cucumbers into pickles; the vinegar's acidity acts as a preservative. The other ingredients are optional and add flavor. You can leave out any you don't like, or try other ingredients like fresh dill, garlic powder, peppercorns, or coriander seeds.

Some pickles are made through the process of fermentation. In the process of fermentation, a chemical reaction occurs through the interaction of the food's sugars and bacteria.

RED CABBAGE
CHEMISTRY

In this experiment, you'll make a pH indicator solution from red cabbage and use the solution to test whether substances are acids or bases.

Step 1

With an adult's help, chop the red cabbage into small pieces on a cutting board until you have about 2½ cups.

MATERIALS

- 2 ½ cups of red cabbage
- 3 clear glasses
- Sharp knife
- Cutting board
- Medium saucepan
- Strainer
- Large measuring cup
- ¼ cup vinegar
- 1 teaspoon baking soda
- Spoon
- Water

Step 2

Place cut up cabbage in a medium saucepan and cover with water. Bring to a boil and then turn off heat. Let cabbage steep, stirring occasionally, for about 25 minutes or until room temperature.

Step 3

vinegar water baking soda

Step 4

Pour the cabbage mixture through a strainer and into a large measuring cup. This dark purple liquid is the indicator solution you will use.

Prepare 3 glasses with your test samples. In the first glass, pour about ¼ cup of vinegar. In the second glass, pour about ¼ cup of plain water. This is neutral, or the control. In the third glass, mix a teaspoon or so of baking soda into about ¼ cup water. Stir until dissolved.

Step 5

Step 6

Pour some of your cabbage indicator solution into the first glass of vinegar. Stir with a spoon and notice the color change. *What color does the liquid become?*

Pour some of your cabbage indicator solution into the second glass of plain water and stir. *Does the color of the liquid change, or does it stay the same purple color as the original indicator solution?*

Step 7

HOW DOES IT WORK?

Pour some of your cabbage indicator solution into the third glass of baking soda. Stir with a spoon and watch the color change. *What color does the liquid become? What would happen if you added more baking soda to the glass?*

Red cabbage contains a pigment called anthocyanin that changes color when it is mixed with an acid or a base. The pigment turns reddish-pink in acidic environments and bluish-green in alkaline (basic) environments. Your first glass turned reddish-pink because vinegar is an acid. Your second glass of plain water didn't change color because water is neutral. Your third glass turned blue because baking soda is a base.

SOAPY SHAKE

Baking soda is a base. Lemon is an acid. See how they react with each other! This can overflow the glass, so make sure you're in an area that can be cleaned easily.

MATERIALS

- Tall glass
- Spoonful of baking soda
- A few squirts of dishwashing detergent
- Lemon juice (½ cup to a cup)
- Food coloring (optional)

Step 1

Drop a few spoonfuls of baking soda into the glass.

Step 2

Squirt some dishwashing detergent on top of the baking soda.

Step 3

If desired, add a few drops of food coloring.
We added red food coloring to ours.

Step 4

Begin pouring lemon juice into your glass. Stir.
As the baking soda reacts to the lemon, a soapy,
bubbly concoction will rise slowly in the glass.

If needed, add more baking
soda or more lemon juice.

HOW DOES IT WORK?

Baking soda is a base. Lemon juice is an acid. When they mix, it creates bubbles of carbon dioxide. The gas bubbles interact with the dishwashing detergent, and you end up with a soapy shake—you can't drink it, but you could clean dishes with it!

INFLATE A BALLOON

Can you inflate a balloon without blowing into it or using a pump? You can if you combine a liquid and a solid to make a gas.

Step 1

Stretch out the balloon before you begin by inflating it fully and then deflating it. This will allow the balloon to more easily expand during the experiment.

Step 2

Use a funnel to add 2 teaspoons of baking soda to the deflated balloon.

MATERIALS

- Balloon
- Empty water bottle
- 2 teaspoons baking soda
- ⅓ cup vinegar
- Funnel

Step 3

Use a small binder clip to close the upper neck of the balloon, leaving enough room at the end to stretch over the bottle's neck.

Step 4

Pour ⅓ cup of vinegar into the empty bottle.

Step 5

Keeping the baking soda in the body of the balloon, carefully stretch the neck of the balloon over the neck of the bottle.

Step 6

Remove the binder clip. Lift the balloon up and allow the baking soda to fall into the vinegar. *What do you observe? How long does it take the balloon to fully inflate? How long does the balloon remain inflated?*

HOW DOES IT WORK?

The balloon inflates because of a chemical reaction between the baking soda (a base) and vinegar (an acid). When the baking soda and vinegar mix, a gas called carbon dioxide, or CO_2, is created. The gas in the bottle has nowhere to go but into the balloon, so the balloon inflates. Similarly, we exhale carbon dioxide when we blow up balloons.

ERUPTING VOLCANO

Make a model volcano and then cause an eruption with a chemical reaction.

- Air-dry clay
- Disposable cup
- Small container
- Paper plate
- Tape
- Cardboard
- Scissors
- Wax paper
- Small dish of water
- Paint
- Measuring cup
- ¼ cup vinegar
- 1 teaspoon baking soda
- 1 teaspoon dishwashing liquid
- Few drops of water
- Red food coloring

Step 1

Tape a small container onto the top of an upside-down disposable cup to form the crater. We are using a 3¼-ounce condiment container on top of a 9-ounce cup.

Step 2

Cut strips of cardboard about 5 inches (12.7 cm) long and 1¾ inches (4.5 cm) wide. Cereal boxes work great. Tape the cardboard strips to the sides of the crater container at the top.

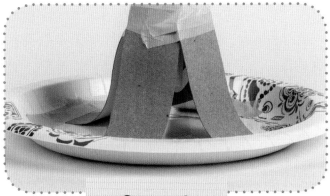

Step 3

Tape the bottom of the cardboard strips to the paper plate.

Step 4

Place wax paper down on your work surface. Scoop out some air-dry clay.

Step 5

Form clay into thin strips by flattening it between fingers or by pressing clay down onto the wax paper and spreading it out.

Step 6

Place clay strips onto the sides of the volcano structure. Dip fingertips in small dish of water and mold volcano pieces together. Use smaller pieces of clay to fill in gaps.

Step 7

Allow clay to dry completely on paper plate. This usually takes 2–3 days. It's okay if it's lumpy or cracked–so are real volcanoes!

Step 8

Paint and decorate volcano as desired. We used 2 coats of brown spray paint. Once paint is dry, you are ready for the eruption.

Step 9

Mix ¼ cup vinegar, about 1 teaspoon of dishwashing liquid, a few drops of water, and a few drops of red food coloring in a measuring cup.

Add 1 teaspoon baking soda to the crater container at the top of your volcano. The paper plate will help keep your eruption mess to a minimum, but it's smart to place the plate on an easily cleaned surface.

Step 11

Quickly pour the vinegar mixture into the crater container with baking soda and watch your volcano erupt!

HOW DOES IT WORK?

The baking soda reacts with the vinegar in the mixture and produces carbon dioxide (CO_2) gas. The gas releases bubbles through the dishwashing liquid and food coloring, creating the bubbly, orange lava that erupts from your volcano.

HEAT AND COLD

Heat is a form of energy, also called thermal energy. When a substance is hot, the atoms and molecules inside it are moving quickly. When a substance is cold, the atoms and molecules inside it are moving slowly.

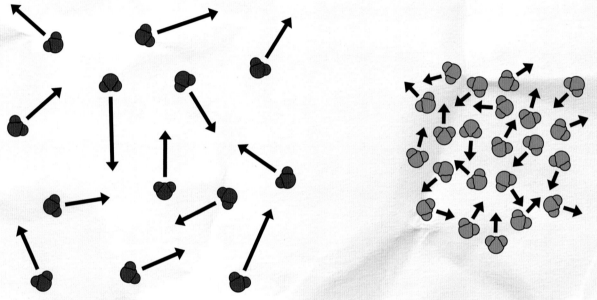

FROM HOT TO COLD

When you put something hot near something cold, the heat moves from the hotter object to the colder object until equilibrium is reached. When heat moves directly from one object to another, it is called conduction. Have you ever touched something metal, like a doorknob, when it is hot outside? You probably pulled your hand away quickly, because it was too hot! Some materials, like metals, conduct heat very well.

Many pots are made of metal to conduct heat quickly from the stove to the food inside the pan. But the handle is usually made of or coated with a material that inhibits the transfer of heat, so you don't burn your hand.

KEEPING COLD

If you've ever eaten a popsicle quickly on a hot day to keep it from melting, you know that keeping something cool can be a challenge. What did people do to store food before they had a refrigerator or freezer? Underground caves and cellars helped people keep food cool so it would last longer.

In the 1800s and early 1900s, many people had iceboxes. Companies collected ice in the winter and stored it. An iceman would then bring a daily shipment of ice to his customers for use in their icebox.

This picture from 1923 shows an iceman making his deliveries.

FISHING FOR ICE

Use a piece of yarn and a little bit of salt to "fish" for ice cubes.

MATERIALS

- Glass of water
- Ice cubes
- Yarn
- Salt
- Stopwatch or timer on a phone

Step 1

Fill a glass with cold water and ice.

Step 2

Rest the yarn on top of the ice. The yarn does not stick to the ice.

Step 3

Pour a bit of salt on top of the ice cubes and yarn.

Step 4

Wait at least 30 seconds.

Step 5

Gently tug on the yarn. This time,
the ice sticks to the yarn.

Step 6   How many ice cubes can you pick up?

HOW DOES IT WORK?

Adding salt to ice changes its freezing point, allowing it to melt and refreeze around the yarn. In areas that get snowfall, people put salt and other materials on the roads and on their driveways to melt the ice and snow and make it safe to drive.

ICE CREAM

You can make your own ice cream.

MATERIALS

- Bowl of ice
- 1 cup of water
- Salt
- Thermometer
- 1 gallon zipper bag
- Smaller zipper bag
- 1 teaspoon vanilla
- ½ cup of sugar

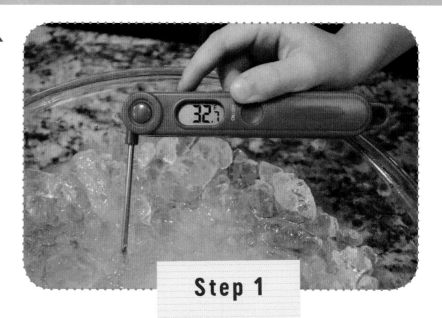

Step 1

Measure the temperature of the ice bowl.

Step 2

Add salt to the bowl of ice.

Step 3

It's colder. Why? The salt lowers the freezing point of the ice.

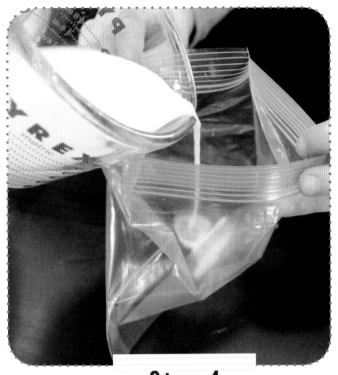

Step 4

Add milk to the smaller bag.

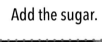

Step 5

Add the sugar.

Step 6

Add the vanilla.

Step 7

Zip up the bag.

Step 8

Add salty ice from the bowl to the larger bag and place the smaller bag inside it and zip it up.

Step 9

Shake and squeeze the bags for 5 to 10 minutes. This prevents the ice crystals forming inside the ice cream from getting too large and keeps your ice cream smooth and creamy.

Step 10

Pull out the smaller bag.

Step 11

You have ice cream!

BAKED...ICE CREAM?

Can a dessert be hot and cold at once? Baked Alaska can.

MATERIALS

- Ice cream
- Plastic wrap
- Glass bowls
- Four eggs
- 2 cups of sugar
- ½ teaspoon cream of tartar
- Chocolate cake
- Ovenproof plate

Step 1

Line a bowl with plastic wrap.

Step 2

Put ice cream in the bowl, smashing it down flat. Put the bowl in the freezer for an hour.

Step 3

Take the ice cream out of the bowl and place it upside down on the cake. The plate you use needs to be ovenproof.

Step 4

Separate the yolks of the eggs from the whites. Discard the yolks. Always wash your hands when handling raw eggs.

Step 5

Beat the egg whites in a mixing bowl until they are frothy. You are making the meringue that goes on top.

Step 6

Add the cream of tartar and whisk the egg whites again.

Step 7

Add the sugar.

Step 8

Continue to beat the mixture until it is shiny and can form stiff peaks.

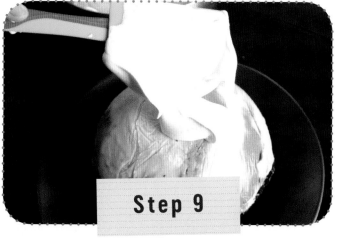

Step 9

Use a spatula to quickly and carefully coat the ice cream and cake with the meringue.

Step 10

Have an adult pop the Baked Alaska into an oven preheated to 450 degrees for three minutes.

Step 11

Using oven mitts, the adult should take the Baked Alaska out of the oven. Let it cool for a minute, then slice into it. Amazingly, the ice cream has not melted!

WHY DOESN'T THE ICE CREAM MELT?

The egg whites contain a protein called albumin. When you beat the egg whites, the albumin molecules rearrange in a way that traps lots of tiny air bubbles. The air bubbles trap the heat, baking the surface of the dessert while leaving the ice cream inside intact.

SOLAR OVEN PIZZA BOX

Foil, dark construction paper, and plastic wrap all help intensify heat energy from the Sun in order to melt food. Try this project on a hot, sunny day.

MATERIALS

- Clean pizza box
- Aluminum foil
- Plastic wrap
- Black construction paper
- Ruler
- Tape
- Scissors
- Marshmallows
- Pencils or pen

Step 1

Draw three sides of a square on the top of your pizza box.

Step 2

Cut along the lines to make a second lid that can be raised and lowered.

Step 3

Wrap the flap with foil. Use tape if necessary.

Step 4

Add foil to the bottom of the box.

Step 5

Add black paper to the bottom of the box.

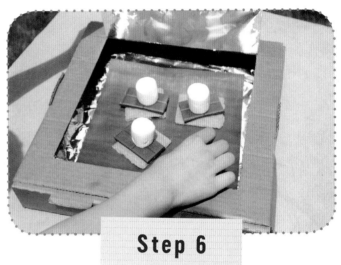

Step 6

Add food. Do not use food that can spoil in heat.

Step 7

Wrap the box in plastic wrap and set it in a sunny spot. Prop open the foil lid with a pencil.

Step 8

The food inside will gradually melt! The plastic wrap traps the heat inside.

POLYMERS AND PLASTICS

A polymer is a special kind of molecule—a very large one made up of chains of smaller molecules that are called monomers. "Poly" is just a prefix meaning "many," while "mono" means one.

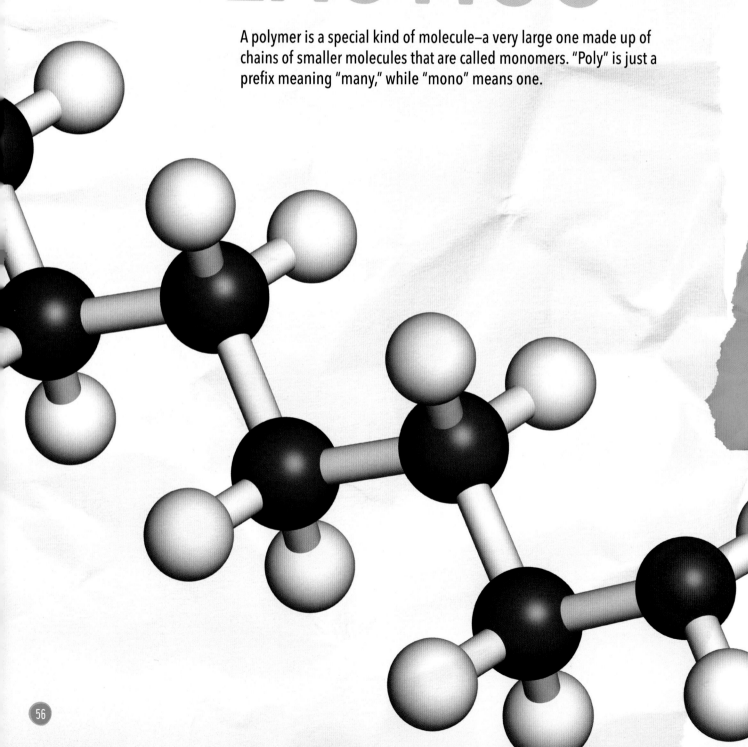

NATURAL POLYMERS

Wool and silk are polymers. The cellulose found in trees and paper is a polymer, too. Proteins are polymers made up of monomers called amino acids.

SYNTHETIC POLYMERS

Inventors began creating synthetic polymers that mimicked natural ones. Sometimes they adapted natural polymers. For example, rubber is a natural polymer, but people began to make modifications to make it more useful. Eventually people began to create fully synthetic polymers such as nylon.

PLASTICS

Plastics are synthetic polymers. They're named for their plasticity—meaning they can be shaped easily. The first plastic, Bakelite, was invented in 1907. Today plastics are everywhere. One worry that people have is that there are too many plastics! They do not degrade easily. People are now working on biodegradable plastics and recyclable plastics.

LEAKPROOF BAG

What do you think will happen when a plastic bag full of water is punctured by pencils?

MATERIALS

- Clear zippered plastic bag
- Pitcher of water
- Sharpened pencils

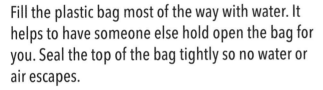

Step 1

Fill the plastic bag most of the way with water. It helps to have someone else hold open the bag for you. Seal the top of the bag tightly so no water or air escapes.

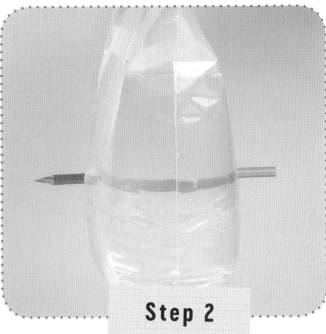

Step 2

Hold the bag at the top with one hand. Push the first pencil, sharpened end first, through one side of the bag and partway out the other side. *Did any water leak out?*

Make sure your pencils are sharpened!

Step 3

Repeat step 2 with the other pencils. *Did any water leak?* When you're done, remove the pencils over a sink or outside.

HOW DOES IT WORK?

The plastic bag is made out of low-density polyethylene, a strong but flexible material. It contains long chains of molecules called polymers. The tip of the pencil slips between the chains without breaking them. The chains' flexible property helps form a temporary seal around the pencil. This allows the pencil to pierce the bag without leaking any water.

MILK PLASTIC

You can make plastic toys out of milk, which contains a protein polymer called casein.

MATERIALS

- Small pot
- Stove
- 2 cups of milk
- 8 teaspoons of vinegar
- Strainer
- Cookie cutters
- Sunny day
- Paint (optional)

Step 1

Pour the milk in a pot.

Step 2

Have an adult heat the milk over medium heat, stirring constantly.

Step 3

Add the vinegar and stir it in.

Step 4

Keep stirring for 1 minute. Curds will begin to form.

Step 5

Strain out the liquids, leaving the curds.

Step 6

Squish out the excess liquid with a spoon.

Step 7

Cut the curds into shapes.

Step 8

Set the curds outside to dry.

Step 9

Decorate with paint!

MILK SWIRL

A drop of detergent creates a beautiful image.

MATERIALS

- A cup of whole milk
- Shallow dish or bowl
- Food coloring
- Dish detergent

Step 1

Pour the milk into the dish, covering the bottom.

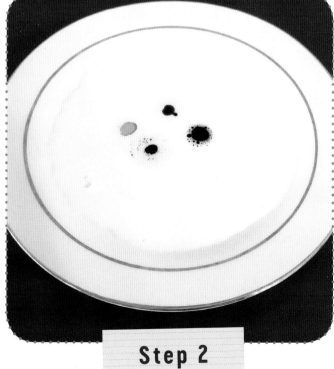

Step 2

Add 4–6 drops of different colors of food coloring near the center of the dish.

Step 3

Add a drop of dishwashing detergent to the center of the dish.

Step 4

The food coloring will begin to react immediately!

Step 5

Watch the milk swirl! *How does the pattern change over time?*

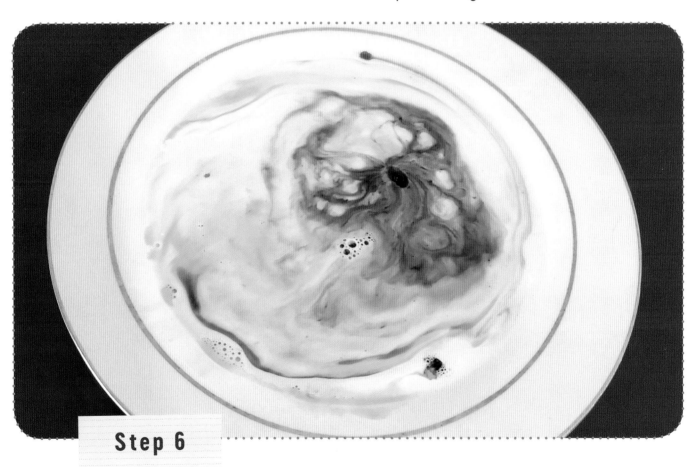

Step 6

Tilt the dish a bit to create a different pattern.

HOW DOES IT WORK?

The detergent breaks up the fat molecules in the milk, creating a colorful reaction. Whole milk works best for this as it has the highest fat content.

NOTES